Essence of English

Nadine Bass

Published by
Brewers Publishing
8 Moat Lane
Melbourn
Royston
Herts
SG8 6EH

First published May, 1998
Reprinted October, 1998

Designed and printed in Great Britain by
Fieldfare Publications, Cambridge.

ISBN 0 9533310 0 8

ACKNOWLEDGEMENTS

My special thanks go to Robert Gibson and Sons, Glasgow Ltd, for permission to use extracts from "Columbus" and "The Lost Race", to the B.M.A. Family Doctor Publications for "Understanding Your Child"; to the Melbourn Magazine for "Recollections of Childhood"; to Random House U.K. Ltd, for three passages from "The Animals Came in One by One"; to John the Poet for "Remedial English"; and to David Higham Associates Ltd, for extracts from "All Creatures Great and Small" and "Watership Down".

I am also greatly indebted to David Grant, M.R.C.V.S. Director of RSPCA Harmsworth Hospital for his kind and ready permission to use the passage from his book "Tales From The Animal Hospital" and to his publishers, Simon and Schuster; also to Orion Books Ltd, in particular to a frantically busy, but extremely helpful, Jean Richardson for permission to use three extracts from "Pet Heroes".

I would also like to thank Pat Birch of the Central Library, Cambridge, for her help with research, and Anne-Marie of Fieldfare Publications for her endless patience and support.

I regret that I have been unable to trace the copyright owner of J. Ewing's "The Normans and Plantagenets" and would welcome any information which would enable me to obtain formal permission to use this piece.

I must offer my deepest gratitude to three special people: My daughter-in-law, Emma, whose magic fingers speedily transformed my frequently-illegible scrawl into a neat little disc, so accurately and patiently;

My dearest daughter, Sophie, who assisted Emma, and aided me in countless tasks, giving invaluable help and encouragement.And finally, but by no means least, my husband Graham, without whose constant support this book would never have been written.

For Graham

CONTENTS

INTRODUCTION

Why this book was written.
For whom it was written.
How to use this book.

Basic English Grammar has become a neglected subject in our schools today. Our children are taught that a Noun is a "naming word" and a Verb is a "doing word"; a passing nod is given to adjectives; conjunctions are largely ignored and pronouns, prepositions and adverbs seldom mentioned.

I have, over the years, taught many children who had difficulty with English, both spoken and written. I have taught the old "O" level Grammar and Literature in a "model" comprehensive school; the "D" stream school leavers at West Dock Avenue (where all the boys wanted to be "deckie-learners" on the trawlers and all the girls wanted to work at Reckitts factory); Dyslexic children and others with various learning difficulties in the remedial department of a Village College and have given personal tuition to numerous children with similar problems.

Throughout these years and widely differing locations, one fact has emerged which seems crucial to me. The children have no encouragement to learn (or, indeed, been taught) the basics of the very language that they use every day!

Many parents cannot afford, or have access to, a coach or tutor to help in this area, but all parents who care, can find or MAKE the time to help their children themselves. (Who better? Who knows your child better than you?)

For those who were given a good grounding in English, this is not difficult. But many parents were not given this basic knowledge of English grammar themselves, so for them, the task of helping their children is considerable. That is why I have written this book, and these parents and their children are the ones I have written it for.

There are five sections of the book.

The first, a history of the language, attempts a brief explanation of why our spelling is so complex and why we have so many words which all mean the same thing.

The second section is Grammar. In this section I have attempted to explain what each part of speech does and how it works. There is repetition, deliberately, because this helps the facts to be digested. There are always examples, generally followed by exercises to reinforce what has (hopefully!) been learnt.

The third section is Punctuation. Difficult perhaps, but essential. I have tried to be as explicit as possible and given, again, many examples and exercises.

The fourth section is Comprehension (understanding) and Recapitulation (revision). To make absolutely sure that children are actually understanding what they read and not simply scanning a passage mechanically, there are twenty questions on each written passage which will require much re-reading of the passage and much concentration upon it before these questions properly can be answered. After this there are seven recapitulation exercises to once again reinforce the Grammar and Punctuation already learnt. A vocabulary question is included in most of the recapitulation exercises which may be a little difficult in some, but which is extremely valuable to the child. In all exercises the use of a dictionary is greatly encouraged, even urged! This section, is, of necessity, a very long section.

The fifth, and final, section of this book is devoted to spelling. It has its own introduction and explanations for its use.

The aim of this book is for the parent to read each little part first, ensure that they thoroughly understand it, and then, using this book as a base, explain it to their child. This will take time and (do not doubt it) a great deal of patience. You will find, as you finally work through the recapitulation exercises, that some of them are becoming quite difficult - use these later. Build up to them slowly. There are plenty of easier ones included. It should take a couple of years to work through the book properly, and by the end of that time the hard or awkward exercises....won't be!

As well as using this book for your "English time", PLEASE encourage your child to read. He (or she) will improve his (or her) vocabulary, spelling and Grammar enormously this way. Also, a child who loves to read will never be lonely! Show an interest in the book he's reading, ask him questions about the story or plot, and about the characters within it. Do not scorn what seems to be a "baby-ish" book to you. He will have chosen whatever he is comfortable with, and if it were "baby-ish" to him he would discard it, in boredom. It is better for him to read and FULLY UNDERSTAND and ENJOY, a simpler book, than to struggle with a "harder" book which he cannot understand or enjoy. Give him time. Remember he is a CHILD.

Try to make your "English time" enjoyable. Create a cosy and relaxed atmosphere. Approach it with the same attitude and interest you would have in a television quiz. No-one watching one of those can resist calling out the answers they know. The Grammar questions are just as enjoyable. This is an opportunity for an intimate "together" time where you and your child are learning together and discovering just how fascinating our language really is.

If you find your patience evaporating, stop. Leave it until another day. Your child will "pick-up" on your frustration and the whole session will become a nightmare for both of you. No-one learns anything in that atmosphere except dread and fear, and your child will never come to love English, or even like it, if he dreads or fears it.

So do not throw this book on the floor, or out of the window, or use it to beat your child senseless with. It is not a very big book so this would take some time, cause your arm to ache considerably and almost certainly lead to mutual resentment!

Use this book instead, as a stepping-off point for a journey of discovery. Exchange ideas and examples with your child - he'll think of many that you haven't thought of - and you will think of many that I haven't thought of. Enjoy yourselves. It is good to learn, and knowledge is a great friend to have. I sincerely hope this book will be a help.

N. J. B. Cambridge, March 1998

Part 1

A Short History of the English Language

A short history of the English language

Before we learn about Grammar, and before we learn spellings, it would help us a great deal to know why we have so many words meaning the same thing, and why spellings are so different, awkward and difficult to learn. The answers lie in the history of our language, so we will begin by taking a brief look at this history.

The language we use today is Modern English, but it is not merely a development from Old English, or Anglo-Saxon as it is often called. It is a much richer language than that, because it contains, has absorbed and continues to absorb, elements from many other languages; the chief ones being Celtic, Latin, Norman-French, Greek and modern European, African, Indian, and American languages.

Whilst this "borrowing" from other languages has given us many more nouns, adjectives, verbs and so on, it is also responsible for giving us a complicated spelling structure. Sometimes words which sound alike, but which are spelt quite differently, owe this confusion to the fact that they have totally different roots. Sometimes, for this same reason, they are spelt alike and have totally different meanings.

The Latin prefix ANTI- means "before"
The Greek prefix ANTI- means "against"

The Anglo-Saxon part of our modern vocabulary includes some of the words in commonest use, such as:

Pronouns
Adjectives
Numerals
Prepositions
Conjunctions
some (but not all) Nouns

In parts of Yorkshire today, when children are playing and choosing who shall be first to "go", they will call "Foggia", "Seggia". These words are pure Anglo-Saxon meaning "first", "second". Until as recently as 40 years ago some shepherds in the Lake District, the Yorkshire Wolds and the Yorkshire Dales used Anglo-Saxon numerals and the counting method based upon the five fingers of one's hand. This was used regularly and inherited generation after generation.

Yan	(1)	Yan-a-dik	(1 + 5)	Yan-a-bob	(1 + 10)
Tyan	(2)	Tyan-a-dik	(2 + 5)	Tyan-a-bob	(2 + 10)
Tethera	(3)	Tethera-dik	(3 + 5)	Tethera-bob	(3 + 10)
Methera	(4)	Methera-dik	(4 + 5)	Methera-bob	(4 + 10)
Dik	(5)	Bob	(10)	Yark	(15)

I have vivid memories, from my childhood in the Yorkshire Wolds, of hearing my own Uncle George count his large flock of Leicesters in this way. He never employed any other method, insisting that this way was infallible since you could never forget where you had counted up to!

Old English, or Anglo-Saxon, place-names are common:

Burgh -	a fort	Edinburgh
Burn -	a stream	Blackburn
Dale -	a valley	Swaledale
Law -	a hill	Sidlaw
Mere -	a lake	Windermere
Stead -	a place	Hampstead

The Romans ruled Britain for nearly 400 years, and since they spoke Latin, many of their words became absorbed into our own language and remain.

Chester or Castra -	a camp	Doncaster, Manchester
Fossa -	a ditch	Fossway
Portus -	a harbour	Portsmouth
Strata -	paved roads	Stratford
Vallum -	a wall or rampart	Walsall

Many English words built up from Latin words or roots and vastly increased our vocabulary. For example:
From the Latin verb Venio Ventum - I come - the following words have been built:

advent	convener	contravene	prevent
circumvent	convent	event	
convene	convenient	invent	

From:

ago, actum	I act	agent, actor
clamo, clamatum	I shout	clamour, proclaim
curro, cursum	I run	current, incur
facio, factum	I make	factor, infect
jacio, jectum	I throw	object, eject, projectile
mitto, missum	I send	admit, promise, missive
moveo, motum	I move	mover, motion, motivate
porto, portatum	I carry	porter, import, export
nascor, natus	I am born	natal, nascent
pello, pulsum	I drive	compel, impulse
plico, plicatum	I fold	pliable, implicit
pono, positum	I place	exponent, position, pose
scribo, scriptum	I write	scribble, inscription
sedeo, sessum	I sit	preside, session
spiro, spiratum	I breathe	inspire, perspire, conspire
teneo, tentum	hold	tenant, retention
venio, ventum	I come	convene, prevent
verto versum	I turn	revert, reverse, adverse
video, visum	I see	provide, visor
voco, vocatum	I call	revoke, vocation

Latin prefixes gave us many more words:

ambi	on both sides	ambiguous,ambidextrous, ambition
ante - anti	before	antecedent, anticipate, antique
bene	well	benefit, benevolent, benison

bis - bi	twice	biscuit, biped, bicycle, binocular
con	with or together	connect, contend, conjunction
ex	out of	export, exclude, example, except, exercize
post	after	postpone, postscript, post mortem, post meridiem
pro	forth or for	profuse, progress, protect, pronoun
trans	across	transfer, transcribe,transgress, transcontinental

Trade names joined our language at this time, for example:

vinum	wine
pondus	a pound
menita	mint
mulus	a mule
discus	a dish or plate

Words from the conversion to Christianity gave us:

angel	bishop	priest	hymn
pope	monk	clerk	alter
font	creed	psalm	disciple

Many of these words, although they reached English from Latin, were Greek in origin and indeed Greek prefixes gave us many more words:

Amphi	on both sides	amphibious, amphitheatre
Anti	against	antipodes, antarctic, antidote
Cata	down	catalogue, catapult, cataract
Dia	two	dialogue, diagonal
Eu	well	eulogy, eulogise, euphony
Pro	before, forth	prologue, proboscis, prophet

The Celtic elements in our language give us words like

bannock	basket	cradle	slogan

darn	kilt	clan	shamrock

We also use Celtic place-names:

Aber	a river-mouth	Aberdeen
Ben	a mountain	Ben Nevis
Kil	a church	Kilmarnock
Dun	a fort	Dunfermline
Inch	an island	Inchmarnock
Inver	a river-mouth	Inverness
Mul	a round hill	Mull of Kintyre

The invaders of Britain brought new languages with them and as they settled here, so their words became absorbed into our own language. The Normans gave us words like baggage, cloak, quay and budget. The Norman-French could not pronounce our letter "W" and substituted "gu" for it instead, so giving us words like brogue, rogue and guarantee. During this time many original English words were lost. Sometimes, however, the English word remained in use alongside its Norman-French equivalent, which is one of the reasons why we have so many synonyms in modern English. For example:

warranty - guarantee	legal - loyal	secure - sure
wile - guile	regal - royal	example - sample
ward - guard	fragile - frail	

In 1066, William the Conqueror invaded England and his Norman-French survived for more than 200 years as the language spoken at the Court, by officials and by the wealthier people. English, as a written language almost disappeared, however, it remained the spoken language of the poorest, common people, the Serfs. The words we still use about the feudal system in our history come to us from this time. For example:

chivalry, courtesy, fealty, homage, castle, tournament.

We also adopted legal words like:

assize, circuit, session, parliament, jury, justice, sue.

Norman architecture and religion also supplied words such as:
pilgrim, friar, tonsure, charity, prior, pity, mercy, chapel.
Hunting and cooking gave us these words:

chase, quarry, venison, brace, beef, veal.

When the knights went off to the Crusades with Richard the Lionheart they brought back with them Arabic and Persian words:

caravan	damask	assassin	coffee
sugar	scarlet	alcohol	
cotton	mattress	algebra	

When the Flemish weavers came to England in the Fourteenth Century they brought Dutch words which we adopted, words such as:

hawker	huckster	spool
tug	tub	pack

Later we gained, also from the Dutch, words like:

deck	skipper	yawl
cruise	yacht	busy
keel	boom	dyke

Finally, from British colonies all over the world and from world-wide British trade we have absorbed many words now in common use. For example:

Indian	bungalow, char, curry, thug
African	canary, guinea, oasis, dervish
American	moccasin, squaw, tomahawk, canoe
Australian	kangaroo, tattoo
Chinese	china, tea, typhoon, kaolin
Hebrew	sabbath, messiah, cherub, seraph, rabbi
Italian	stanza, canto, opera, pasta, pizza

German	poodle, quartz, lager, waltz, zinc
Portuguese	caste, cobra, marmalade, fetish
Spanish	alligator, cargo, cigar, grandee, mosquito

Also we have words derived from the names of people or places. (Many surnames are really place-names).

spaniel	herculean	tantalise
amazonian	sandwich	tarmac
guillotine	dunce	utopian
volcano	wellington	cardigan

Space forbids any deeper study, but I hope this peep at the way our words have formed; at their origins and history, may help to explain in a small way, why Modern English is such a complex, fascinating, rich and wonderful language.

If particular words intrigue you, your dictionary will help you to find out the history behind those words. Do, please, use it.

Part 2

GRAMMAR

VERBS (Doing Words)

Verbs are "doing" words, that is, they are the words we use for all actions. Verbs are the words which state whether somebody or something does or is or has anything. Verbs tell us what is happening, what has happened, and what is going to happen. We call this the present, past and future "tense" of a verb. For example:

The woman is knitting socks.	(present tense)
The woman knitted socks.	(past tense)
The woman is going to knit socks.	(future tense)
The sun is setting.	(present tense)
The sun has set.	(past tense)
The sun is going to set.	(future tense)

A verb may also ask a question. For example: Are you happy? Shall we go now? A verb may also give a command. For example: Leave the house! Be quiet! Leave me alone!

Certain verbs are used to express the various sounds made by animals. For example:

Pigs grunt, cats purr, horses neigh, doves coo, dogs bark, owls hoot, donkeys bray, monkeys chatter, sheep bleat, crows caw, hens cluck, ducks quack, lions roar, mice squeek, wolves howl, turkeys gobble, hounds bay, bears growl, geese hiss.

If we put "to" in front of a verb (to skip) we call this the "infinitive", or the "verb infinite".

If we add "ing" to the end of a verb (skipping) we call this the "present tense".

If we add "<u>-ed</u>" to the end of a verb (<u>skipped</u>) we call this the "<u>past tense</u>".

If we add the words "<u>shall</u>" or "<u>will</u>" to the verb, we form the "<u>future tense</u>".

Some verbs do NOT add -ed in the past tense, so we call these "**IRREGULAR**" verbs. Verbs which DO add -ed in the past tense are called "**REGULAR**" verbs.

Here are some examples of REGULAR VERBS. They all end with "-ed"

walk	**walked**	soil	**soiled**	float	**floated**
hop	**hopped**	start	**started**	laugh	**laughed**
jump	**jumped**	stop	**stopped**	cry	**cried**
talk	**talked**	look	**looked**	live	**lived**
shout	**shouted**	wait	**waited**	die	**died**
call	**called**	dance	**danced**	like	**liked**
play	**played**	bounce	**bounced**	hate	**hated**
travel	**travelled**	sail	**sailed**	love	**loved**

Write the past tenses of the following **REGULAR** verbs:

skip	cook	whisper	sew	knit
paint	work	rub	spell	move

Here are some examples of **IRREGULAR** verbs. <u>None</u> end with "-ed"

run	**ran**	seek	**sought**	drive	**drove**
creep	**crept**	swing	**swung**	fly	**flew**
sing	**sang**	throw	**threw**	swim	**swam**
sleep	**slept**	fall	**fell**	do	**did**
read	**read**	grow	**grew**	be	**was**
write	**wrote**	draw	**drew**	make	**made**
think	**thought**	sink	**sank**	light	**lit**
find	**found**	eat	**ate**	see	**saw**

Write the past tenses of the following **IRREGULAR** verbs:

buy shoot drink slay blow
sit sting leap shake slink

All verbs, whether they are regular or irregular have "to" in front when they are infinite. For example:

He is going to sleep. (irregular, slept)
She knows how to knit. (regular, knitted)
She likes to dance. (regular, danced)
The children love to play. (regular, played)
He had to leave immediately. (irregular, left)
Ask them to write to me. (irregular, wrote)
Tell him to hurry up. (regular, hurried)
Please try to find it. (irregular, found)
I would like to drive please. (irregular, drove)
She had to laugh at the kitten. (regular, laughed)

Where "to" is part of the infinitive, it is a fault of style, known as a split infinitive to put any other word or words between "to" and the rest of the infinitive.

WRONG: Mrs Busybody likes to maliciously repeat all the gossip she hears.
CORRECT: Mrs Busybody likes to repeat maliciously all the gossip she hears.

Write out the future and present tenses of the following verbs:

run love think speak hope

Verbs are very important words because they are the words we use to explain what it is we are doing, want to do, have already done, or want other people to do. Without verbs, our speech would make no sense at all. The word "verb" in Latin , means "word". If we put a dash where we would normally use a verb, we cannot understand the sentence. For example:

I ______ you to______ and ______ . I ______ very excited because I ______ ______ ______ ______ my new bike. Will you ______ and ______ me if you ______ ______ ______ ? I ______ ______ forward to it. It ______ ______ brilliant ______ ______ you again!

Now we will put back the missing verbs and we will be able to understand what is being said.

I **want** you to **come** and **stay**. I **am** very excited because I **have learnt to ride** my new bike. Will you **write** and **tell** me if you **will be coming**? I am **looking** forward to it. It **will be** brilliant **to see** you again!

Write out the following passage and underline 20 verbs.

The next time you visit the seaside, try to spend a little time beachcombing. Notice the special whiteness of the pebbles constantly washed by the salty water, and feel the deep green rubbery seaweed clinging to the tide-line. In small rock-pools you may spy Sea Anemones which open and close and sway with each ripple of the water. If you put your finger into the mouth of the Sea Anemones you will feel tiny suckers cling to it. Should you be very lucky, you may discover small Starfish washed ashore during storms that took place out at sea. There may be lots of different shells to collect and sort into various kinds and colours and you may even find interestingly-shaped pieces of drift wood.

Write out the following sentences filling each gap with a suitable verb.

A regiment of soldiers ________ down the road.
________ off the grass.
The birds ________ a nest.
A soldier ________ a uniform.
________ you ________ the news?
The children ________ on the lawn.
Christopher Columbus ________ America.
She ________ the dishes.

AUXILIARY VERBS

Often we find that verbs are helped by "little verbs", which we call Auxiliary Verbs. When this occurs the complete verb may consist of:

The main verb plus one or more Auxiliary Verbs.

The word "Auxiliary" means helpful to, and so Auxiliary verbs are helpful to other verbs. In the sentence

I have been reading this book.

The main verb is reading, and the words HAVE BEEN are Auxiliary Verbs. Thus the verb in this sentence is HAVE BEEN READING; that is, three words make one complete verb.

Here is a list of Auxiliary Verbs:

be	will	must	have	do
is	would	may	has	does
am	shall	might	had	did
was	should	can	were	could

Remember that these verbs are not always Auxiliary verbs - they are Auxiliary verbs when they help other verbs. Sometimes they stand by themselves and form complete verbs, as in:

I had two books in my desk.
Scrooge never did.

Now we have discovered how much we need verbs to communicate with each other, and we have learnt about the verb infinite, the present, past and future tenses of verbs, and we know the difference between Regular and Irregular verbs. We also understand the use of Auxiliary verbs.

The first rule of English Grammar is that "every sentence MUST contain a verb." The shortest sentence in our literature is contained in the Holy Bible. It has just two words. Jesus wept. Although there are only two words in it, it is, nevertheless, a complete sentence. Why? - Because it contains a verb! It also contains a Noun, and now we are going to learn about Nouns.

NOUNS (Naming Words)

The first words we learn to say are name-words or Nouns, such as Mummy, Daddy, drink, and so on. If we visited a different country, where a different language was spoken, and we wanted to make our needs known, again, it would be the Nouns which we would need to learn and use. Nouns are the most essential words in any language.

There are four kinds of **Nouns:**

1. Common Nouns
2. Proper Nouns
3. Abstract Nouns
4. Collective Nouns

<u>COMMON NOUNS</u> are name-words which apply to classes of people (farmers, sailors, ladies, children etc.), places (countries, cities, rivers, mountains etc.), or things (boats, chairs, houses, animals, toys etc.).

"Man" is the name-word given to all men all over the world. They share the name in Common, so the word "Man" is a **Common Noun** - like window, door, table. Common Nouns are the most numerous name-word in our language, therefore there should be no need to use that over worked word "thing". Please try to avoid using this word, because it shows a lack of vocabulary. Use a suitable Noun instead.

Some examples of **Common Nouns** are:

door	plate	cake	towel	chair	shed	flower
car	book	cup	water	soap	cooked	spade
coat	bike	floor	potato	bed	walls	sink
tree	shoes	train	baby	head	arms	legs
field	grass	animals	birds	tree	clothes	sky
clouds	stars	planets	shells	fish	beach	sand
shop	motor	mill	fire	air	soil	lake

PROPER NOUNS belong to a particular person or place, and always have a capital letter.

All the Days of the Week,
All the Months of the Year,
All the Towns and Cities,
All the Rivers and Countries of the World are Nouns, also
All Peoples' Names are Nouns. We call all these Nouns "**Proper Nouns**".

Some examples of **Proper Nouns** are:

London	Paris	Sun	Moon	Monday	Mississippi
August	David	Thursday	Mediterranean	East	Thames
Janet	North	South	West	Himalayas	France
England	January	America	India	Asia	Russia

So the word "city" is a Common Noun, but "London" is a Proper Noun.

Common Noun	**Proper Nouns**
dog	Labrador, Alsation, Poodle, Collie
tree	Willow, Birch, Oak, Ash, Holly
river	Thames, Seine, Ouse, Severn, Trent
country	France, England, Germany, Greece
boy	Jack, Charlie, Jason, Neil, Simon
girl	Lucy, Rosie, Daisy, Chloe, Sophie
mountain	Andes, Himalayas, Alps, Pennines
lake	Ullswater, Como, Michigan, Lugano

ABSTRACT NOUNS are name-words for qualities and feelings which we cannot see or hear or touch. We know these qualities and feelings exist, however, so we need to have a name for them, and this is why we call them **Abstract Nouns**.

Here are some examples of **Abstract Nouns**

happiness	anger	freedom	justice	health
courtesy	sadness	guilt	goodness	truth

honour	rudeness	mercy	peace	beauty
cruelty	pleasure	light	kindness	sickness
strength	weakness	unkindness	darkness	safety
love	hatred	courage	friendship	despair
joy	hope	excitement	dread	anger

We can see when someone is angry. We may hear them shout - but we cannot actually see, or hear, or touch anger itself, because is an abstract feeling. Another word we use for feeling is emotion. The name-words we give to all our emotions are **Abstract Nouns.**

COLLECTIVE NOUNS are the name-words we give to groups or collections of things, people, animals or birds. They are rather interesting, but we do not use them as often as we use the other Nouns.

Here is a list of examples of Collective Nouns:

flock of sheep
archipelago of islands
herd of deer (or cattle)
shoal of fish (or herring)
company of shareholders
library of books
staff of teachers
drove of bullocks
farrow of young pigs
bunch of grapes
crew of sailors
bevy of birds (or girls)
galaxy of stars
pride of lions
horde of barbarians
school of sharks (or whales, or artists)
host of locusts

muster of recruits

draft of soldiers
cabinet of ministers
fleet of ships (or cars)
constellation of stars
swarm of bees (or wasps)
colony of ants
collection of stamps
litter of puppies (or kittens)
brood of chicks
force of policemen
guild of craftsmen
batch of loaves
regiment of soldiers
hatch of chicks
covy of partridges
pack of hounds
flight of finches (or pigeons, or stairs)
gang of stevedores (or ruffians)

gaggle of geese
throng of merrymakers

den of thieves
troupe of minstrels (or actors)

senate of representatives
troop of horsemen (or monkeys)
brace of pheasants
band of musicians

We can have fun making up our own **Collective Nouns.** What about a "giggle of girls" or a "herd of caravans?" Because these **Nouns** are the name-words for a number of things or people collected together, we call them "**Collective Nouns**".

1. Write the following sentences filling the gaps with suitable **Nouns.**

A sweet-natured ________.
Twenty jolly ________.
The fertile ________.
The hardworking ________.
A thick, bushy ________.
The tired, patient ________.
Seven even lines of ________.
A remarkably untidy ________.

2. Write out the following passage underlining all the **Nouns.**
3. State what kind of **Noun** each one is:

Harry felt great excitement as he approached the Circus. He wondered whether he would see the elephants, because they were his favourite animals. Although they were huge and powerful, Harry loved them for their intelligence and patience. Maybe the troupe of clowns would be rehearsing? He liked Topoff best because his face looked so sad. As Harry was musing, the string of prancing, Palomino horses came from their stables into the field beside the Big Top. They formed a circle and began to perform many clever tricks in response to the crack of their trainer's whip.

Now that we have looked at the four kinds of **Nouns; Common Nouns, Proper Nouns, Abstract Nouns**, and **Collective Nouns** - it is time to look at the gender of Nouns.

GENDER OF NOUNS

Nouns and Pronouns may be Masculine (Male), Feminine (Female), Common Gender (either masculine or feminine), or Neuter (belonging to neither sex). For example:

	Masculine	Feminine	Common	Neuter
Nouns	man	woman	voter	table
Nouns	boy	girl	person	book
Nouns	master	mistress	friend	cup
Pronouns	he	she	they	it

Common Gender nouns apply in circumstances where one cannot say whether a Noun is Masculine or Feminine because it could be either - words like:

servant	child	relative	teacher	companion	colleague
student	pupil	customer	patient	victim	driver

All of these people could be male or female so they share a **Common Gender.**

Neuter Nouns are easy to remember because they name things without life! Just think of them as the names of objects, as:

table	door	school	piano	toy	pen
chair	house	car	coat	ship	plate

It is the Masculine and Feminine nouns which we need to think about, because they are often totally different words. We can recognise the ones which do not change easily enough, as:

Masculine	Feminine	Masculine	Feminine
shepherd	shepherdess	poet	poetess
host	hostess	heir	heiress
landlord	landlady	emperor	empress

but very often nouns have separate words for the Masculine and Feminine versions and we need to know these; not simply for the sake of our vocabularies, or even for our general knowledge, but because the use of the correct word in speech and writing, makes our meaning much clearer for our listener, or reader. Here is a list of **Masculine** and **Feminine** nouns, some of which change words, some do not. Some will be unfamiliar, many will be familiar. Use your dictionary to find the meanings of any unfamiliar words.

Masculine	Feminine	Masculine	Feminine
hero	heroine	bachelor	spinster
monk	nun	widower	widow
abbot	abbess	uncle	aunt
marquis	marchioness	earl	countess
sir	madam	lord	lady
duke	duchess	sultan	sultana
testator	testatrix	executor	executrix
czar	czarina	fox	vixen
bull	cow	buck	doe
ram	ewe	stag	hind
gander	goose	drake	duck
billy-goat	nanny-goat	manservant	maidservant
lion	lioness	tiger	tigress
negro	negress	author	authoress
god	goddess	bridegroom	brid
prophet	prophetess	baron	baroness
actor	actress	nephew	niece

Pick out the **Nouns** from the following passage, and opposite each write its **gender.**

The girl came with her brother on a visit to their Uncle. They saw geese and hens in the farm-yard, whilst the dairy-maid was busy making butter. Many people passed along the road.

Give the <u>**feminine**</u> form of:

gander	marquis	poet	sultan
author	hero	fox	earl

NOUNS FOR YOUNG ANIMALS

The young of a dog is called a puppy. Here is a list of Nouns which name the young of other animals.

pig - piglet
horse - foal
rabbit - kitten
sea-lion - calf
goose - gosling
frog - tadpole
cow - calf
hen - chick
fox - cub
lion - cub
antelope - faun
rhinoceros - calf

swan - cygnet
hare - leveret
eel - elver
goat - kid
elephant - calf
seal - pup
whale - calf
duck - duckling
bear - cub
salmon - fry
giraffe - calf

donkey - foal
ostrich - chick
kangaroo -joey
deer - faun
badger - earthpig
cat - kitten
eagle - eaglet
sheep - lamb
tiger - cub
zebra - foal
hippopotamus - calf

SINGULAR AND PLURAL NOUNS

Nouns are said to be **singular** when they refer to one person, place or thing; they are said to be **plural** when they refer to more than one. Thus, "window" is singular, but "windows" is plural. Collective nouns are sometimes regarded as singular, sometimes as plural. For example:

The **team** plays best on heavy ground. ("Team" is regarded as a single unit).

The **team** have every confidence in their captain. ("Team" is regarded as a number of individual players, so is therefore plural in this sentence).

To form the plural:

1) **Add "S"**

hymn - hymns
yacht - yachts

2) Nouns ending in a hissing sound **add "ES"**:

gas - gases
glass - glasses
church - churches
ditch - ditches
box - boxes
fox - foxes

3) Nouns ending in f or fe:

Add "S"

dwarf - dwarfs
cliff - cliffs
roof - roofs
chief - chiefs
reef - reefs

Change "F" into "V" and add "-ES"

knife - knives
loaf - loaves
wolf - wolves
thief - thieves
wharf - wharves
scarf - scarves

4) Nouns ending in "y":

With a vowel before the "y", **add "S":**

chimney - chimneys
donkey - donkeys
valley - valleys
boy - boys

With a consonent before the "y", change the **"Y" into "I" and add "- ES"**:

lady - ladies
pony - ponies
daisy - daisies
city - cities
spy - spies
duty - duties

5) Nouns ending in "O":

Add "S"	**add "-ES"**
bamboo - bamboos	cargo - cargoes
cameo - cameos	echo - echoes
curio - curios	hero - heroes
folio - folios	motto - mottoes
photo - photos	negro - negroes
piano - pianos	potato - potatoes
solo - solos	tomato - tomatoes

6) Add "**-EN**":

ox - oxen	child - children

7) **Change vowel sound:**

man - men	woman - women
mouse - mice	goose - geese
foot - feet	gentleman - gentlemen
tooth - teeth	dormouse - dormice

8) **Nouns which are unchanged:**

sheep - sheep	deer - deer
salmon - salmon	trout - trout

9) **Words borrowed from other languages:**

radius - radii	crisis - crises
axis - axes	maximum - maxima
basis - bases	minimum - minima
oasis - oases	phenomenon - phenomena
gateau - gateaux	plateau - plateaux

10) **Compound words:**

court-martial	courts-martial

father-in-law	fathers-in-law
son-in-law	sons-in-law
man-servant	men-servants
woman-servant	women-servants
looker-on	lookers-on
man-of-war	men-of-war

11) **Nouns with NO SINGULAR:**

bellows	shears	measles	billiards
trousers	scissors	mumps	draughts
compasses	pincers	tongs	soapsuds
knickers	underpants	shorts	jeans

12) **Nouns with two plurals:**

brother - brothers, brethren	die - dice, dies
cloth - cloths, clothes	penny - pence, pennies

All these lists are simply examples. There are many exceptions which are best not learned from rules, but from careful observation.

Write down the **plural** of each of the following words:

chief	manservant	his	child
thief	chimney	that	pony
ox	radius	axe	fly
deer	daisy	German	negro
Dutchman	table-cloth	scarf	spoon

Write down the singular form of each of the following words:

oases	volcanoes	geese	calves
ladies	knives	sheep	hippopotami
minima	crises	dormice	yachts

PRONOUNS

Pronouns are very useful, short words which are used instead of, or in place of, Nouns. Although they take the place of Nouns, they are not naming words, which as we know, Nouns are. Pronouns are used instead of name words and in this way they help us to make sentences without repeating the same word. If the word stands by itself in a sentence, it is a **pronoun**.
Jane is clever, but Jane does not boast. Here we have too many Janes! If we use the Pronoun "**she**" we can avoid this repetition.

Jane is clever, but she does not boast. The Pronoun "she" stands in place of the noun, "Jane".

Joe saw the lion and Joe stared at the lion. Again, we have repetition. Too many Joes and too many lions. We will use the Pronouns "**he**" and "**it**" and create a much smoother and more interesting sentence. Hence:

Joe saw the lion and **he** stared at **it.** The pronoun "he" stands in place of the noun "Joe", and the Pronoun "it" stands in place of the Noun "lion".

There are four kinds of **PRONOUNS.** They are:

Personal Pronouns
Relative Pronouns
Demonstrative Pronouns
Interrogative Pronouns

PERSONAL PRONOUNS

I	mine	we	us	he
me	you	ours	yours	she
they	his	hers	theirs	it
him	her	them	one	others
myself	himself	herself	each	everyone

everybody anyone anybody my

Here are some examples of how we might use these **Personal Pronouns:**

Everyone attended the school sports day. Jack and I were to enter several races. He was nervous, but everyone told him not to worry. I felt rather nervous myself, since my sister Jane's race was before mine and we would admit to anyone that ours was not an athletic family.

One could see them lined up for their start, tense and waiting. Suddenly they were off! It was a very fast race, with each runner giving her level best, and Jane acquitted herself well. Anybody could see that she was trying hard, but the others were well in front of her. Jack and I cheered her on, his voice almost as loud as mine. Gradually we realized that Jane was catching up quite noticeably and Jack, turning to me, said "It's because of us shouting and encouraging her!" He felt proud of Jane's effort himself, and called loudly to my sister as she ran past us "You can win! The race is yours!".

RELATIVE PRONOUNS

Relative Pronouns also stand in place of nouns, but they are used to **join** two sentences together.

This is the jumper, Grandma made it. (note "it" is a personal pronoun).
This is the jumper **that** Grandma made.

"That" is the **Relative Pronoun** which has now joined the two sentences together and it relates to the noun "jumper". **Relative Pronouns** should always be written as near as possible to the noun to which they relate.

Relative Pronouns are:

who whose whom which that what where

We use "who" and "whom" for people; "which" for things, and "that" and "whose" for both people and things.

Here are some examples:

This is the boy. The boy climbed the tree.
This is the boy **who climbed the tree.**

The pupil gave a note to the teacher. It was addressed to the teacher.
The pupil gave a note to the teacher **to whom** it was addressed.

I met the boy. His puppy was playful.
I met the boy the boy **whose** puppy was playful.

Here is the meadow. A stream runs through it.
Here is the meadow through **which** a stream runs.

We looked through the magazine. We wanted to buy it.
We looked through the magazine **that** we wanted to buy.

This is the wood. Bluebells grow in the wood.
This is the wood **where** Bluebells grow.

DEMONSTRATIVE PRONOUNS

Demonstrative Pronouns are used to indicate, or show, what is being referred to.

They are:

this that these those

Here are some examples of how we use **Demonstrative Pronouns:**

This chocolate is good, but **that** chocolate is better.
These sweets are yours, but **those** sweets are mine.

"These" is the plural of "this", "those" is the plural of "that". The **Demonstrative Pronoun** must always agree with the Noun it relates to. If the Noun is singular, the Demonstrative Pronoun must also be singular. If the Noun is plural, the Demonstrative Pronoun must be plural. It would be quite wrong to say:

Those hat is black, but these hat is red.
This hats are black, but that hats are red.

The two sentences are wrong because their nouns and Demonstrative Pronouns do not agree. Say why they do not agree, then write out the sentence with the nouns and Demonstrative Pronouns **agreeing**, first in the singular, then in the plural form.

INTERROGATIVE PRONOUNS

The word "interrogative" means questioning. We call a lengthy session of questioning an "interrogation". So **interrogative pronouns** are the ones which ask a question.

Interrogative Pronouns are:

who? which? what? whose?

Some examples are:

Who did you visit yesterday?
Which picture did you like best?
What are you doing?
Whose pen is this?

Now we have learnt that just as there are four kinds of Nouns, there are four kinds of Pronouns. These are **Personal Pronouns, Relative Pronouns, Demonstrative Pronouns** and **Interrogative Pronouns.**

Write out these sentences filling the gaps with suitable **Pronouns**, and say what kind of Pronoun you have used.

Take your coat and I'll take ________.
You take my book and I'll take ________.
________ have left ________ in the lurch.
Has ________ left the house?
________ cried, "Give ________ food!"

Join each pair of sentences to make one, using either "who" or "which".

This is a pen. I bought this pen yesterday.
Daisy has a brother. He is a soldier.
I have a remedy for 'flu. I can recommend it.
This is the wood. I found Primroses in it.
The girl wears a blue coat. She took my message.

ADJECTIVES

Adjectives are describing words. They describe, and add meaning to, Nouns and Pronouns. They also answer the question "what kind of?".

"Hat" is a common noun. We want to know "what kind of" a hat? Here are several **adjectives** to answer our question and describe the hat to us.

An old, floppy, grey comfortable hat.
A pretty, blue, summer, straw hat.
A warm, red, knitted, woollen hat.
A smart, black, formal, bowler hat.

If we were to think of our English language as a painting, we might decide that our Nouns and Verbs would be the pencilled outline sketch of whatever we were going to paint, however, it would be our enormously rich adjectives which would provide us with all the fascinating colours that we would need to use, to make our painting truly beautiful.

We can "paint" word-pictures which make the listener or reader feel sad, happy, fascinated or thoughtful, by choosing the appropriate adjectives and by using lots of them. Or, by not using any adjectives at all, we can bore our listener or reader so much that they will lose interest in whatever we are saying or writing. If we do not use adjectives to describe nouns and pronouns when we are speaking or writing, then whatever we want to say becomes a mere list of facts or a bland and boring report, and not nearly as interesting as it would have been had we used adjectives.

Adjectives help us to use our imagination and to visualize whatever is being described. Think about an angry sea, a towering mountain, a red-gold sunset, a starlit night and crunchy autumn leaves. Much more interesting, don't you think, than simply sea, mountain, sunset, night and leaves?

Adjectives really are helping words for nouns and pronouns, because they also show us numbers or amounts. One bike, sixty bikes; some sweets, several sweets.

Adjectives can have three forms or degrees. These are called the **Positive** Degree, the **Comparative Degree** and the **Superlative Degree.** The degrees of adjectives help us to describe more precisely whatever we are

talking or writing about, and so convey our meaning more clearly to our listener or reader.
Here are some examples:

Positive	Comparative	Superlative
tall	taller	tallest
fine	finer	finest
brave	braver	bravest
wise	wiser	wisest
wealthy	wealthier	wealthiest
bold	bolder	boldest
true	truer	truest
late	later	latest
ripe	riper	ripest
small	smaller	smallest

Some adjectives change words when their degree is altered. For example:

Positive	Comparative	Superlative
bad	worse	worst
much	more	most
good	better	best
little	less	least

For longer adjectives we add the words "more" and "most".

Positive	Comparative	Superlative
beautiful	more beautiful	most beautiful
wonderful	more wonderful	most wonderful
ambitious	more ambitious	most ambitious
thoughtful	more thoughtful	most thoughtful

The **Comparative** Degree of the adjective is used when two things or sets of things or people are compared:

Alan is **taller** than Sophie.
London is **bigger** than Cambridge.

The <u>**Superlative**</u> Degree of the adjective is used when more than two things or people are compared:
Alan is the **tallest** of them all.
London is the **biggest** city in Britain.

Complete the comparison (degrees) of these adjectives.

Positive	**Comparative**	**Superlative**
great	________	________
hot	________	________
________	larger	________
________	drier	________
________	________	happiest
horrible	________	________
________	sillier	________
________	________	most jealous
________	sloppier	________
________	________	closest

Always try to <u>avoid</u> using the words "<u>nice</u>" and "<u>sweet</u>". They are <u>vague</u> words and show a lack of vocabulary. It is far better to <u>use an adjective</u>. We are very fortunate, because our English language is particularly rich in adjectives. The word "nice" is usually used wrongly. It's real meaning is "precise". There are other frequently-used vague words which should be avoided, among them are:

nasty awful bad super brilliant smashing horrible dreadful

It is usually laziness that encourages us to be satisfied with vague words. If we like the weather, we call it vaguely "nice weather", when by using an exact adjective we could express precisely what we like about it; for example, fine weather, warm weather, sunny weather. In the same way, when we dislike the weather we may be lazy and call it bad weather, or nasty weather, or horrible weather or dreadful weather. None of these vague adjectives expresses exactly what we dislike about the weather, whereas with a little thought we could easily find one that does so. For example: wet weather, foggy weather, cold weather, misty weather, muggy weather, close weather, oppressive weather. If, for instance, you are content to call your friend "nice" you cannot be bothered to find the word that truly expresses your feeling towards your friend. He or she might be liked for being kind, honest, reliable, helpful, instructive, amusing, handsome, pretty, well-read, intelligent, gentle, musical, sporting, energetic, strong-minded, tolerant, frank, modest, generous, or many other things. It would be far better to describe your friend in one or more of these ways.

Use each of these exact adjectives to replace one of the *italicised* vague adjectives in the sentences below:

discordant rude sunny considerate slow deep quick
exhilarating

It was a *nice* day yesterday.
We had a *brilliant* swim.
Your brother seems to have a *bad* temper.
The knife inflicted a *nasty* wound.
It was *sweet* of you to lend me your book.
His behaviour was *awful.*
How *dreadful* her singing is!
I am t*errible* at learning maths.

Replace each of the following vague adjectives by at least three adjectives, each of which tells us exactly what kind of journey etc.,

an awful journey	a terrible headache
a super player	a dreadful hat
a brilliant dinner	a smashing picture

Write the following sentences replacing the words "nice" and "sweet" with carefully chosen adjectives.

Sophie is a sweet girl and has nice hair.
It was a nice beach, with nice trees growing nearby.
This is a sweet picture of your sister.
We will make lots of nice presents.

That is a nice Christmas tree!
Wales is a nice place to visit and the people there are sweet.
That lady is wearing a sweet hat.
This is a nice baby and her dress is sweet.
Fiona has a sweet kitten, it is really nice.
I am reading a nice book which has sweet illustrations.

Certain **Adjectives** are made from **Nouns**, often Nouns which name qualities. It is always interesting to notice the change made to the meaning of a word by the addition of a few letters, for example:

Nouns	Adjectives	Nouns	Adjectives
west	western	warmth	warm
hope	hopeless	height	high
beauty	beautiful	kindness	kind
tact	tactful	goodness	good
fame	famous	justice	just
courage	courageous	wisdom	wise
industry	industrious	activity	active
ignorance	ignorant	hardihood	hardy

Write down the adjectives made from these nouns:

winter	ignorance	electricity	Autumn
punctuality	commerce	custom	nature
truth	child	caution	fear
misery	hero	mountain	grief
gratitude	fury	haste	deceit
man	disaster	quarrel	gold

ADVERBS

An **Adverb** is a word which qualifies, or modifies, a verb, an adjective, or another adverb. Qualify and modify mean "add to the meaning of" something, so **Adverbs** describe verbs, adjectives or other adverbs in the same way that adjectives describe, or qualify, nouns and pronouns. **Adverbs** are used for asking questions such as: How are you? Where are you going? When will he leave? Why does he not speak? All these adverbs qualify verbs, but clever adverbs also answer questions for us, by telling us how the action of a verb was done, or where, or when. For example:

The dog barked **savagely**. Savagely is the **Adverb** which tells us how the dog barked. So we say that "savagely" is the adverb qualifying the verb "barked".

I am coming <u>now</u>. "Now" is the adverb telling us when I am coming "Now" is the adverb qualifying the verb "coming".

He walked slowly. "<u>Slowly</u>" is the adverb qualifying the verb "walked".

The girl was <u>very</u> beautiful. Very is the adverb qualifying the adjective "beautiful."

Adverbs should be placed **next** to the verb they qualify. For example:

They leapt <u>simultaneously</u> over the wall and <u>instantly</u> disappeared from view. How did they leap? Simultaneously. Simultaneously is the **Adverb** qualifying the verb "leapt" and is placed next to it. How did they disappear? Instantly. Instantly is the adverb qualifying the verb "disappeared", and again, is placed next to it.

There are <u>five</u> kinds of adverbs. They are:

Adverbs of time
Adverbs of place
Adverbs of manner
Adverbs of degree
Adverbs of number

ADVERBS OF TIME are the Adverbs which tell us - when?
I met him <u>recently.</u>
He left <u>yesterday</u>.
I <u>seldom</u> see him.
He went <u>early</u>.
She went <u>today.</u>
I visited her <u>frequently</u>.

ADVERBS OF PLACE are the Adverbs which tell us - where?

He went <u>yonder</u>.
I saw him <u>there</u>.
She went <u>below</u>.
The school is <u>above</u> the village.

ADVERBS OF MANNER are the Adverbs which tell us - How?

The Thrush sang <u>clearly</u>.
He went <u>cheerfully</u> to school.
She <u>hastily</u> climbed the fence.
He walked <u>slowly.</u>
She gazed <u>thoughtfully</u>.

ADVERBS OF DEGREE are the Adverbs which tell us How much? or "To what degree?" These Adverbs qualify or modify <u>adjectives</u> or other Adverbs, rather than verbs.

The ship approached <u>very</u> slowly. "Very" qualifies the adverb "slowly".
The ship approached at a <u>very</u> slow speed. "Very" qualifies the adjective "slow".
He went <u>very</u> cheerfully. Here is an adverb added to another adverb showing us not <u>how</u> he went, but how <u>cheerfully</u> he went; that is, the word 'very' tells us the degree of his cheerfulness.

They worked <u>fairly</u> carefully. An adverb added to another adverb showing us how carefully they worked. The word "fairly" tells us the degree of their carefulness.

ADVERBS OF NUMBER are the Adverbs which tell us "How often?" or "Which are?"
The officer repeated his instructions twice.
The twenty-third psalm.
The second turning on the right.
I have written this seven times.

Adverbs, like adjectives, may be used in three degrees, Positive, Comparative and Superlative. Adverbs normally form the Comparative by adding "more" and the Superlative by adding "most". Jack is careful and Mary is more careful but Henry is the most careful. Here are some examples of comparison of adverbs:

Positive	Comparative	Superlative
strongly	more strongly	most strongly
happily	more happily	most happily
willingly	more willingly	most willingly
foolishly	more foolishly	most foolishly

Write the following sentences replacing the gaps with suitable **Adverbs**.

________ did you hide the money?	(place)
The child snuggled ________ into the warm bed.	(place)
________ must you leave now?	(degree)
A rabbit ________ popped up by the hedge.	(manner)
He jumped up and ________ welcomed us.	(manner)
She is going home ________.	(time)
I will explain for the ________ time.	(number)

Now that we have studied adverbs we can see that, like adjectives, they help to make our sentences more interesting and colourful.

CONJUNCTIONS

Conjunctions are joining words, which we use to join single words, groups of words, or sentences together. For example:

He could not budge the door, **though** he tried again and again; **but** the next man opened it easily.

Boys and girls <u>often</u> play together.
The Sun is shining <u>but</u> it is still cloudy.
The cat <u>and</u> her kittens cuddled up together.
I shall go home <u>unless</u> you stop me.

Six <u>and</u> four make ten. (Here, the conjunction AND joins two words, six and four). We left <u>as</u> he arrived. (Here, the conjunctioln AS joins two sentences. We left. He arrived). We use the conjunctions "and" and "but" most frequently. Here are some more **conjunctions:**

for	even so	either	than	because
although	until	nor	that	so
while	unless	neither	or	if
also	whilst	after	when	before
where	whether	as	since	lest
in case				

The word "like" is NOT a conjunction and should **never** be used as a joining word. It would be quite wrong to say "I knit like my mother taught me". We use the conjunction "as", which is correct. Hence, "I knit <u>as</u> my mother taught me".

Conjunctions may be used to join:

Two nouns:	Jack <u>and</u> Jill went up the hill.
Two verbs:	He came <u>but</u> was sent home again.
Two Adjectives:	The lady was infirm <u>and</u> old.
Two adverbs:	The girls wrote neatly <u>and</u> well.

Sometimes three or more words are joined together, then we use commas, and only one AND is necessary.

Jack <u>and</u> Tom played	(two nouns joined)
Jack, Tom <u>and</u> Charlie played	(three nouns joined)
Jack, Tom, Charlie <u>and</u> Fred played	(four nouns joined)

Here is a passage written by a girl, aged 10 years. She has not used conjunctions, therefore her sentences tend to be a little jerky. Notice how often she uses the word "got", which should be avoided whenever possible. "Has got" is bad grammar. We need only to use the word "has".

"The cottage has got a thatched roof. It has got a brown wooden door, and it has the number ten written on the door, with gold metal. The cottage's walls are painted a snow white colour. The cottage has a crooked old chimney that's got bricks missing from it. The cottage has got ivy growing up its walls. One of the windows has got a little stained glass pattern on it".

Let us look at the same passage which has been written, using conjunctions. You may feel that it not only flows more fluently, but that it has also become more interesting.

The cottage has a thatched roof and also a brown wooden door with "Number Ten" written upon it in gold metal. The walls of the cottage are painted a snow-white colour whilst the crooked old chimney has bricks missing from it. The cottage has ivy growing up its walls and one of the windows has a little stained glass pattern upon it.
(Thankyou to Fiona for this.)

Write out the above version of the passage, and underline <u>five conjunctions</u>.

Join all of the following pairs of sentences with a conjunction:

You must take an umbrella. It is raining.
He tried to stand. He was too weak.
The child must stay here. Her mother returns.
I will go now. You will promise to stay.

I cannot understand. He does not come.
The woman cleaned the house. Her husband was at work.
He locked the door. He put the key in his pocket.
We will take the hamper. We will have a pic-nic.

Write out the following sentences, filling the gaps with conjunctions.
Your house is larger ________ mine.
The man ________ his son were seen in the car.
You can walk ________ ride.
I know ________ you are an honest man.
I cannot tell ________ he is speaking the truth.
She lay down ________ slept.
Do not buy something ________ it is cheap.
You will not succeed ________ you work hard.

Now we understand conjunctions and we have learnt six parts of speech. These are: **verbs, nouns, pronouns, adjectives, adverbs** and **conjunctions.** To make sure that we properly understand them all, here is a short exercise:
Write out the following sentences, filling each gap with a suitable word, and stating what part of speech the word is. (e.g. noun, adjective, conjunction, verb, adverb).

He left the level ground and ________ the hill.
________ make their nests in trees.
As she was ________ tired, she lay down.
I shall not return ________ you send for me.
The child hid ________ the cupboard.
I have a ________ Persian kitten.
________ are you going now?
Have another ________ of tea before you go.
Jenny is coming and ________ brother is coming too.
He was wearing a ________ blue coat.

PREPOSITIONS

A **preposition** is usually a little word standing in front of a noun or pronoun, so introducing a phrase. Its main work in the sentence is to show the relationship between these nouns or pronouns and other words or groups of words. Because the position of these little words is pre- or before, a noun or pronoun, we call them prepositions. Here are some of the simple **prepositions:**

above	across	after	against	at
behind	beside	below	between	by
down	during	over	through	for
until	upon	with	from	in
round	around	outside	inside	of
before	beneath	under	into	off
to	on	up		

Here are some examples showing the work of **prepositions:**

The leg **of** the table. Here, the little preposition "of" shows the relation between the "leg" and "table".
The hole **in** the wall. In this case, the preposition "in" shows the relation between "hole" and "wall".

Here are some more examples of the use of the preposition. The *italics* will help you to see how each preposition shows the relationship between two words.

The *plane* **above** *us* is about to land.

The *path* **through** the *wood.*

They *rolled* **down** the *hill.*

We *looked* **round** the *corner.*

Place the *book* **upon** the *table.*

He was *good* **at** *games.*

Amy *went* **to** *school.*

"Between" is used when two people or things are indicated. For example:
Divide the cake between Tom and Jack.
Between a rock and a hard place.

"Among" is used when more than two things are indicated. For example:
Divide the cake among the children.
He is one among many.

Certain verbs need special **prepositions** as their relating-words:

similar **to**	accomplished **in**	dependent **on**
different **from**	compared **with**	independent **of**
differ **from**	rebel **against**	

We need to learn these, because if we give any of these verbs different prepositions from the ones which belong to them, we will be guilty of using bad grammar!

The preposition usually comes before the noun or pronoun to which it is most closely related, so the noun or pronoun which comes after a preposition, is called its object, as:

I left the book upon the table. Here the noun "table" is the object of the preposition "upon". A preposition always has an object.

Here are some commonly-used phrases with their prepositions. We can call them "**Prepositional Phrases**".

at any rate	on the whole
at your service	by no means
for dear life	in black and white
to his heart's content	in the lurch
by dint of	to all appearances

in spite of   for the most part

Write the following sentences filling the gaps with **prepositions.**

There were a lot of marbles ________ the bag.
Shrimps live ________ water.
Elephants live ________ land.
This coat is different ________ that one.
It was greatly ________ his credit.
He was sent to prison ________ life.
The canoe floated ________ the river.
Take your hat ________ the peg.
A wall ran ________ the town.
The letter was delivered ________ special messenger.

Read the following passage, noticing the prepositions.

Dusk was falling as I wandered down the lonely lane to the farmhouse. After a while, I was surprised to hear a murmur of voices drifting through the twilight. The sound seemed to be coming from across the field beside, and slightly below, me. I continued along the lane, sloping gently downwards now, beneath the arching branches of the whispering trees which lined either side of it. The sound of voices grew a little and I distinctly heard a peal of joyous laughter which seemed to come from inside the trees, through which I could see twinkling lights, and a kind of shadowy flickering, as though flames were dancing. As I strolled round a bend in the lane, I came suddenly upon a gypsy caravan, drawn up beside the hedge.

How many <u>different</u> prepositions are there in the above passage?
Write a list of all the prepositions in the above passage, naming each one once.
Which preposition is used most frequently in the passage?
How many times does the writer use this preposition?
Which preposition beginning with "b" is used twice?

SIMILE

When we are describing something we often use a phrase such as "like a whirlwind" or "as lovely as a rose". A word-picture of this kind is called a **simile.** You can recognise similes very easily because they are usually preceded by "like", "as" or "as if".

A good simile should not only make the meaning of a sentence more vivid, it should also add beauty to the whole expression. The poet Wordsworth wrote "I wander'd lonely as a cloud", the words "as a cloud" make his description more vivid and help us to understand how solitary he was.

A bad simile would be: "The pale, yellow sun gleamed in the sky like the unbroken yolk of a fried egg". In this example, the sun, one of Nature's greatest glories, is compared with something trivial and ordinary and the whole effect is ludicrous.

We use similes so frequently that we often forget to make up our own, even though original similes are much more interesting. Here are some examples of commonly-used similes:

When his misdeeds were discovered Jack turned as red as a beetroot.
Sitting quite calmly, she remained as cool as a cucumber.
The children were so late they ran like the wind.
He took to school like a duck to water.
Her talent shone like a star.
Showing no affection, she was as cold as ice.
She brushed and brushed her hair until it was as soft as silk.
She was as brown as a berry when she returned from her holiday.
After the sports, Tom was as hungry as a hunter.
He fainted, and fell like a stone.

Write the following sentences filling the gaps with a suitable **simile.**

As thin as ________ .

The heavy bundle dropped like ________ .
The dragon's eyes glowed like ________ .
As quiet as ________ .
The sky was tinted like ________ .
As good as ________ .

As well as being introduced by "like" or "as", similes are sometimes introduced by "as if". For example: He staggered about as if he were drunk. She spoke to him as if he were a fool.

We have looked at a list of commonly used **similes**, and you will be able to think of many more examples yourself, but in creative writing , it is much more imaginative and therefore much more interesting , to use your own similes. Like adjectives, they lend colour to your desciptions.
Try to make the following ideas vivid and imaginative by creating your own similes.

A person you meet once but never see again.
A vast field of corn waving in the wind.
A wild rush of a crowd of people.
A meadow full of wild flowers.
An angry sea.
Someone singing very sweetly.
Fields seen from an aeroplane.
A very proud person.
A very sun-burnt person.
Someone moving very rapidly.

Sometimes we use a repetition of the same consonent sound. We call this **alliteration.** Apart from creating particular effects, alliteration makes words memorable. Hence many proverbs and similes make use of it;

Like a wolf in the fold.
As cool as a cucumber.
Like a bolt from the blue.
As clear as crystal.
As busy as a bee.
As bold as brass.
As dull as ditchwater.

METAPHOR

We have seen how similes make word-pictures using the words "like" or "as" or "as if", but sometimes the word-picture is made leaving out the words "like" and "as" and we call this **Metaphor.**

A **Metaphor** is a figure of speech in which one thing or person is identified with another because of a resemblance in some way. For example:
King Richard was brave.
The lion is known to be brave.
King Richard is, therefore, called Lion-Heart.

When we call Richard "The Lion-Heart" we are using a **Metaphor.**

<u>THE DIFFERENCE BETWEEN SIMILE AND METAPHOR.</u>

A simile says one thing or person is LIKE another, that is, it <u>compares</u>.

A Metaphor says one thing or person IS another, that is, it <u>identifies</u>.

As in:
The ship of state needs a steady hand on the wheel.

Life is but a walking shadow.

A **Metaphor** is a condensed form of simile, and is therefore often so much more concise, that it is useful to be able to condense similes into metaphors. For example, the **simile**

"She is like a spiteful cat" is more concise when we change it to a **Metaphor** and say "She <u>is</u> a spiteful cat".

Simile Silence is like gold for its value.
Metaphor Silence is golden.

Simile	For many hours the fire behaved like a man in a rage.
Metaphor	For many hours the fire raged.
Simile	He guided the state as a pilot does a ship.
Metaphor	He was the state's pilot.
Simile	He was as strong as a lion.
Metaphor	He was a lion.
Simile	They crossed a lawn like velvet.
Metaphor	They crossed a velvety lawn.

Re-write the following sentences changing the similes to **Metaphors.**

The sky was tinted like a rose.
He whistled like a bird.
She brushed hair that was like a raven's wing.
Their dresses were as white as snow.
The blow descended like lightning.
The battle raged like a storm.
He ploughed a furrow as straight as an arrow.
Her voice was like a cold blast of wind.
He was a ship that passed in the night.
The poor tramp was as lean as a rake.

The purpose of Metaphor, like that of simile, is to make speech and writing more vivid and interesting. Metaphors are best used sparingly, however, otherwise you will lose their effect.

A possible Metaphor for "a clumsy person" would be "A bull in a china shop", just as "The ship of the desert" is a Metaphor for a camel.

Explain the meaning of the following **Metaphors:**

Play second fiddle.
The apple of his eye.
A red letter day.

Sour grapes.
The last straw.
Bury the hatchet.
A flash in the pan.
A tower of strength.

PROVERBS

A proverb is a concise statement which expresses well known truths. Proverbs are traditional expressions, handed down from one generation to another. Proverbs are worded in figurative language. For example, when we say "people who live in glass houses shouldn't throw stones", we really mean that people who can be criticised themselves, should not criticise others. "Rome was not built in a day" means that it takes time to accomplish a great task.

Every language has short pithy sentences known as Proverbs. Here are some examples from the English language.

A bird in the hand is worth two in the bush.
A friend in need is a friend indeed.
A rolling stone gathers no moss.
A stich in time saves nine.
All that glistens is not gold.
All work and no play makes Jack a dull boy.
All's well that ends well.
Beggars cannot be choosers.
Birds of a feather flock together.
Do not count your chickens before they are hatched.
Enough is as good as a feast.
Well begun, well done.
Cut your coat according to your cloth.
Every cloud has a silver lining.
Forwarned is forarmed.
Half a loaf is better than no bread.
Honesty is the best policy.
It takes two to make a quarrel.
Least said, soonest mended.
Look before you leap.
Make hay while the sun shines.
Many hands make light work.
More haste, less speed.
Necessity is the mother of invention.

Never look a gift horse in the mouth.
Out of debt, out of danger.
Too many cooks spoil the broth.
Where there's a will there's a way.
Waste not, want not.
Don't cross your bridges until you reach them.
It's a bad workman who blames his tools.
Possession is nine-tenths of the law.
Give him an inch and he'll take a yard.
A drowning man will clutch at a straw.
In the country of the blind, the one-eyed man is king.
Strain at a gnat and swallow a camel.
When the cat's away the mice will play.

Write in your own words, the meaning of the following proverbs:

A bird in the hand is worth two in the bush.
Fine feathers make fine birds.
Beauty is only skin deep.
Discretion is the better part of valour.
Like father, like son.
Empty vessels make the most sound.
One swallow does not make a summer.
He who pays the piper calls the tune.
It never rains but it pours.
Out of the frying-pan into the fire.

The sense of one proverb sometimes contradicts the sense of another. Here are six proverbs. For each one, write another opposite in meaning:

Out of sight, out of mind.
Too many cooks spoil the broth.
He who hesitates is lost.
There's many a slip between the cup and the lip.
Better late than never.
Bad news travels fast.

PREFIXES and SUFFIXES

It is very common in English to attach a particle (or group of letters) either to the beginning or to the end of a word to alter or modify its meaning, for example:

Pleasant, UNpleasant, UNpleasantNESS

A particle attached to the beginning of a word is called a Prefix, one attached to the end of a word is called a Suffix.

Prefixes

mis	im	pre
dis	ir	circum
un	ig	auto
in	non	sub
il	ante	arch

The first nine prefixes above (mis to non) are Negative Prefixes, that is, they mean"not" or "the reverse of". The prefix 'in' often has the second letter changed to make the word easy to pronounce, as in Perfect, Imperfect. Remember that in adding the prefix mis- or dis- you never get a double "s" unless the word to which you are adding already begins with an "s"; e.g. fire - misfire; please - displease; but spell - misspell; satisfy - dissatisfy.

Dis- Distrust (cannot trust), Disappear (not to appear, vanish)
In- Inconvenient (not convenient), Indiscreet (not discreet or prudent)
Il- Illegible (not legible, not easily read), Illegal (not legal)
Im- Improper, Impossible, Impersonal
Ir- Irregular (not regular)
Ig- Ignoble (not noble or honourable), Ignore (take no notice of)
Mis- Mistrust (not to be trusted), Misunderstood
Non- Nonsense (not sense), Non-stop (does not stop)
Un- Unruly (not obedient to rules), Unsteady.

Form new words from these by using the prefix dis- or mis-. check your answers with a dictionary.

doing	connect	continue	understand
arm	believe	place	arrange
direct	deed	comfort	demeanour
courage	fortune	spell	state

Pre means before, as in Premature, Prefix (fixed before).
Circum means round, as in circumference.
Auto means self, as in automaton.
Sub means under, as in subordinate.
Arch means chief, as in archangel.
Ante means before, as in anteroom

Form new words from the following by using the prefix ante- or pre-. Check your answers with a dictionary.

position	amble	date
natal	mature	caution
destination	determine	diluvian
judge	sentiment	chamber

Write one word for each phrase, inserting the necessary Prefix:

One's own signature (__________graph).
Bad luck (__________chance).
To sail round the world (__________navigate).
Lower layer of rock (__________stratum).
Motor car (__________mobile).
Under water (__________merged).

Suffixes:

en	some	ible	ock
on	ful	fy	let

ness	able	ling	et
less	kin	ette	

Prefixes or Suffixes may be used to form verbs e.g.:

short shorten
prison imprison

Suffixes may be used to form adjectives, for example:

trouble troublesome
beauty beautiful
laugh laughable
sense sensible

Some adjectives are made opposite in meaning by adding the suffix "less".

less hopeful hopeLESS

Diminutive suffixes help to form the names of small creatures or things (like -let in "hamlet"). Common diminutive suffixes are -t, -et, -ette, -let, -ling, -en, -kin and -ock. As in:

ling	duck	duckling
en	chick	chicken
ock	hill	hillock
let	brook	brooklet
et	lance	lancet
ette	cigar	cigarette

Notice the word "solidify". It is built up of two parts: solid plus fy. The suffix "fy" comes from the Latin word "facio", which means "make" or "make into". The word solidify thus means: make solid. Form words ending in "fy" from the following and check your answers with the dictionary.

horror unit pure diverse

terror	liquid	revive	intense
class	false	code	crucifix
null	stupid	clear	peace
vile	type	rate	saint

There are a great many more examples of prefixes and suffixes in the spelling section of this book.

HOMOPHONES

There are some words which cause difficulty and confusion because they sound alike but are spelled differently; these words are called Homophones. The best way to understand their differences is to note how they are used in sentences. Here is a selection:

dependent (Adjective) - depending on.
dependant (Noun) - the person who depends on another.
envelop (Verb) - to wrap up.
envelope (Noun) - a cover for a letter.
lee - the side sheltered from winds.
lea - a meadow or field.
legible - can be easily read.
eligible - fit to be chosen for a particular position.
illegible - cannot easily be read.
mantel - a shelf above the fireplace.
mantle - a cloak.
medal - a piece of metal in the form of a coin.
meddle - to interfere.
mustard - a yellow plant, used as a condiment.
mustered - called together, congregated.
practice (Noun) - the actual doing of anything.
practise (Verb) - to do often.
license (Verb) - to allow, to give permisson.
licence (Noun) - permission, paper giving permission.
principle - a rule or doctrine.
principal - chief.
angle (Noun) - the corner where two lines meet.
(Verb) - to catch fish with a rod.
angel - a spirit.
prey (Noun) - animal or bird hunted by another.
(Verb) - to plunder, to cause anxiety.
pray (Verb) - connected with prayer.
whether - whether you win or lose.
weather - the weather is fine today.
To - A Preposition and therefore followed by a

noun.		Also used with verbs (to think, to fall, etc.) Come to tea. I have come to visit you.
Too	(Adverb) -	Means also, more than enough. You must come, too. I have eaten too much.
Two	(Adjective) -	The number which comes after one, and before three. Come at two o'clock. There are two cakes left.
Here	-	Here come the boys. I will meet you here.
There	-	There are many flowers. He is over there.
Their	-	Belonging to them. Indicates possession and belongs to the same family as our, your. You can place the word "own" after it without altering the meaning of the sentence. They will come in their car.
Where	(Adverb) -	Indicates place. Where are you going?
Were -		Belongs to the verb "to be". We were going home.
So	(Conjunction) -	Means therefore. We finished our work, so we left.
Sew	(Verb) -	To stitch, with a needle and thread.
Are	-	Are you coming? There are many different trees.
Our	-	Indicates possession. It is our dog i.e. it belongs to us.
No	-	Negative. I have no money. No, thank you.
Know	(Verb) -	To be aware of, to learn, to be acquainted with. I know all about it. I know my tables. I know her well.
Your	-	Belonging to you. Bring your books with you. I like your shoes.
You're	-	You are. You're coming, too. You're a very good swimmer.
Colonel	-	A military rank. You must salute a Colonel.
Kernel	-	The edible inside of a nut.
Yew	-	A yew tree.
Ewe	-	A female sheep.
Goal	-	How many goals did you score?

Gaol		-	The prisoner was sent to gaol (jail).
Coarse		-	It is very coarse cloth. Means rough.
Course		-	Of course. A race-course. A course of study.
Herd		-	A herd of cattle or deer.
Heard	(Verb)	-	To hear. I heard you calling.
Dying		-	The plant was slowly dying.
Dyeing		-	I am dyeing this cloth a different colour.
Profit		-	Gain or benefit.
Prophet		-	One who foretells the future.
Rain		-	Water falling from clouds.
Reign		-	To rule, the period of rule.
Rein		-	Long narrow strap used in driving a horse.
Residents		-	Inhabitants, not visitors.
Residence		-	A dwelling.
Site		-	Ground on which a town or building stands or
is to			be built.
Sight		-	Connected with vision or seeing.
Stationery		-	Writing material sold by a stationer.
Stationary		-	Fixed, still, immoveable.
Story		-	A tale or narrative.
Storey		-	The first, second etc. floor of a building.
Unanimous		-	All of the same opinion.
Anonymous		-	Without the name of the writer or doner.
Vain		-	Having too high an opinion of oneself, useless.
Vein		-	A blood vessel, a seam of coal in rock.
Vane		-	A weathercock.
Yoke		-	A piece of wood placed across necks of oxen or men to assist in carrying.
Yolk		-	Yellow part of an egg.
Advise	(Verb)	-	To give an opinion.
Advice	(Noun)	-	The opinion so given.
Affect		-	To pretend, to move or touch, to love.
Effect		-	The result or consequence of something.
Assent		-	To agree.
Ascent		-	The act of climbing.
Bail		-	Placed on cricket stumps.
Bale		-	A package.

Birth		-	The origin or beginning.
Berth		-	The cabin on a ship.
Chews		-	Breaking up food with the teeth.
Choose		-	To select, decide.
Decent		-	Fitting, right, respectable.
Descent		-	A downward slope.
Guest		-	A visitor.
Guessed		-	He guessed the time as he had no watch.
Key		-	The key belongs to this lock.
Quay		-	The boats were anchored at the quay.
Boy		-	A young male. The boy admired his father.
Buoy		-	A navigational aid.
Night		-	It was a quiet, starry night.
Knight		-	A knight in shining armour.
Desert		-	The sands of the desert.
Dessert		-	The pudding or sweet.
Threw	(Verb)	-	The boy threw the ball.
Through		-	I saw it through the window.
Sold		-	The baker sold all his bread.
Soled		-	Shoes are soled at the shoe repairer's.

The following words are grouped in pairs of **Homophones.** Using a dictionary, write down each of their meanings.

write	pair	pier	brake	right	cheque
wright	pear	peer	break	write	check
ceiling	horde	gate	maze	peddle	role
sealing	hoard	gait	maize	pedal	roll
bier	faint	gambol	pain	heir	aisle
beer	feint	gamble	pane	air	isle
serial	martial				
cereal	marshall				

Which words in brackets should be used to fill the blank spaces in the following sentences?

The train went at_______ minutes_______ _______. (to, too, two).
It was_______ that the kittens lost _______ mittens. (their, there).
We_______ going _______ the smiths _______ living. (were, where).
Of _______ you will go. (coarse, course).
_______ hats were found over _______. (their, there).
The men _______ from the pier. (angel, angle).
The stone went _______ with _______ parents. (their, there).
They _______ the _______ of cattle coming. (heard, herd).
The prisoners of the _______ scored a _______. (goal, gaol).
_______ did that_______ on your mind? (prey, pray).
The _______ boys went _______ the orchard once _______ often. (to, too, two).
We ate chocolate,_______ cakes and ice cream _______. (to, too, two).

HOMONYMS

You have just learned that words which are identical in pronunciation, but different in spelling, are called Homophones.

There are other words in English which are identical in spelling and pronunciation, but are different in meaning. For example, in the phrases "a tent pole", "the North pole", the word pole is used in two entirely different senses. Such words are called Homonyms.

Here is a list of Homonyms. For each word write two sentences illustrating its different meanings:

file	grate	hue	mail
ball	quail	bark	rock
smack	bore	fire	

SYNONYMS

Synonyms are pairs of words with approximately the same meaning. For example:

jeering and mocking
clever and intelligent
stormy and tempestuous

Write as many words as you can, similar in meaning to these:

see	gift
happiness	clever
sorrow	traveller

Write down the following words in a single column. Opposite each, write a suitable **synonym**.

answer	authentic	flower	alter
attempt	expensive	celebrated	frighten
client	repudiate	detach	gallant

From the group of words in the second column, choose a **synonym** for the single word in the first column. A dictionary will help you.

fickle	firm, feeble, changeable, constant
rudeness	audacity, hostility, incivility, contention
speed	volley, contrive, project, velocity
injure	exaggerate, impair, diminish, obstruct
destroy	demolish, impede, undermine, intercept
scatter	descry, disperse, dispel, erase
entice	persuade, plead, invite, lure
hinder	stop, reject, impede, prevent

Each word in the first column has a **synonym** in the second. Pair them off.

daring	shelter

unnoticeably	edible
vanquish	audacity
eatable	temperate
equable	defeat
refuge	imperceptibly
confirm	ratify

Synonyms, though having roughly the same meaning, often have a quite different use. For example, "beaming" and "twinkling" are synonyms. They both mean "shining", but although we might describe a searchlight as beaming, we would not describe a beaming star. In the same way we might say "a twinkling star" but we would not say a "twinkling searchlight" because it would not make sense.

Here is a list of synonyms. Use them in sentences of your own to bring out the shades of difference in their meanings.

famous	celebrated	notorious
eminent	noteworthy	notable

Pair off the <u>nouns</u> in the following lists with their <u>most appropriate adjectives</u>.

<u>Shine</u>

sparkling	dial
glowing	jewels
glittering	tinsel
flickering	glow-worm
glistening	water
gleaming	heat-haze
luminous	candle
shimmering	dewdrops

<u>Noise</u>

cooing	rivulet
cawing	reed
whispering	bowstring
sighing	dove
warbling	breeze
twanging	rook
howling	blast
screeching	chains
clanking	glass
tinkling	owl

For a word to be a true synonym, it must be the same part of speech as the word it replaces, hence, a synonym for a noun must be a noun; a synonym for a verb must be a verb, a synonym for an adjective must be an adjective and so on. If this rule is not followed, the word you are using as a synonym will not be a true synonym.

ANTONYMS

Antonyms are pairs of words with approximately the opposite meaning. For example:

clever	and	stupid
ugly	and	beautiful
deserted	and	crowded.

Put together the words which are opposite in meaning:

opaque	lengthy
liquid	rough
dainty	mean
brief	depressing
friend	cheerful
amusing	transparent
generous	clumsy
despondent	enemy
smooth	solid

Write as many words as you can opposite in meaning to these:

temporary	captivity
love	always
soften	enormous

Write down the following words in a single column. Opposite each, write a suitable Antonym, without using prefixes:

take	inhale	sly	monotonous
build	ahead	steep	hinder
approach	calm	futile	attack

In each of the following groups of words there are three Synonyms and one Antonym. By making sure of the meaning of all the words in the group, (using a dictionary) pick out the Antonym.

1. courtesy, politeness, inconsiderateness, civility.
2. belittle, flatter, under-estimate, disparage.
3. grave, facetious, jocular, bantering.
4. placid, peevish, irritable, petulant.
5. interpret, confuse, expound, explain.
6. maim, mutilate, mar, remedy.
7. repeal, confirm, rescind, annul.
8. endorse, ratify, confirm, question.
9. congress, assembly, dispersal, conference.
10. delegate, individual, deputy, representative.

We learnt that synonyms have different shades of meaning, and the same is true of antonyms. Although you may be able to think of several words opposite in meaning to each *italicised* word below, you will find that there is only one which is exactly right for the sentence in which it is used. Use this **exact Antonym** for each italicised word:

The metal *contracted* when the temperature *fell.*
The man has an *unpleasant* personality and a *crude* sense of humour.
The engine ran *loudly* and the exhaust pipe was *deafening.*
He repeated *monotonously* that his friend was i*ntoxicated.*
Noisily the smoker *inhaled.*
Her *imaginary* friend was an *excitable* child.
The *numerous* workers *hindered* one another.
Because of his *rudeness*, people *despised* him.
The *boisterous* puppy *infuriated* the *irritable* old man.
She was *frequently* given *disapproving* looks.

Pair off each phrase in the first column with one of opposite meaning in the second column.

out of work	under cover
over a long period	by slow degrees
in a dilapidated state	in a short space of time
by leaps and bounds	in a regular job
in the open	in good condition

ENGLISH IDIOMS

Every language has certain figurative expressions peculiar to itself. These expressions are called Idioms. For example, "a bolt from the blue" is an idiomatic phrase or expression. An idiomatic way of saying that a man is living up to the limit of what he can afford is to say that "he has as many dogs as he has bones for."

A good knowledge of the idiom of any language is a great asset in speaking and writing that language. The following is a list of idiomatic expressions for you to become familiar with:

to draw the long bow
to draw a bow at a venture
a cock and bull story
a storm in a teacup
the thin end of the wedge
to show the white feather
a last-ditch stand
sail close to the wind
run with the hare and hunt-
with the hounds
draw in one's horns
send someone to Coventry
the window's mite
the Benjamin of the family
a white elephant
a wild goose chase
to play a double game
to play to the gallery
cutting off his nose to spite his face
to strike while the iron is hot
to take the bull by the horns
within bounds
by all accounts
to set the teeth on edge
to cast aspersions

a flash in the pan
out of the frying pan into the fire
to go from bad to worse
Hobson's choice
a busman's holiday
cheeseparing economies
the last straw
eat the leek

eat humble pie
a red herring
take pot-luck
to burn one's boats
to burn the candle at both ends
French leave
to keep his own counsel
to throw in the sponge
to sit on the fence
to turn over a new leaf
to kick over the traces
to stand firm
to the utmost
in the open air
to see the light of day
on the face of it

out of doors
to make its appearance
to the highest degree
to catch a glimpse of
at first sight
having a finger in many pies
to be hauled over the coals
kicking against the pricks
crying for the moon
courting disaster
to set one's wits to work
on the sly
to publish abroad
a snake-in-the-grass
under one's nose
to cudgel one's brains
to sail under false colours
to tip the wink
the scales fall from one's eyes
not to mince matters
by word of mouth
with all one's heart
to keep mum
in all its detail
on paper
by all means
to beat about the bush
to heave in sight
by and large
to catch one's eye
taken up with
to refuse to hear
in the main
to appear on the horizon
when all is said and done
to turn a deaf ear to
to be uppermost in one's mind

hot enough to roast an ox
within reason
to all intents and purposes
with bated breath
to jar upon the ear
facing the music
having too many irons in the fire
carrying coals to Newcastle
riding like Jehu
before one's eyes
for your eyes only
give the eye
to have one's eyes opened
to commit to writing
a sheep in wolf's clothing
to hold one's tongue
to place on record
to drag into the limelight
on no account
having the gift of the gab
in a nut-shell
never say die
in the open
to keep it dark
to blurt it out
with an ill grace
unable to put two words together
all things considered
to engross one's thoughts
to take note of
the mind running on other things
to have all one's wits about one
to bear in mind
to raise its ugly head
at the end of the day
to attract one's attention
to keep a sharp look-out

to keep cavey
to be hell-bent on
one's thought being elsewhere
in no way
to be intent upon
riding hell-for-leathe
by hook or by crook
by no means

Choose ten of the idiomatic expressions above, and write out each one in a separate sentence of your own to show that you understand its meaning.

LAZY AND INCORRECT GRAMMAR

We have already learnt that it is lazy to use the verb "get" and its past tense "got", when we could employ so many verbs in their place. Get and got are vague verbs and will spoil your speech and writing.

In the same way, the words "nice" and "sweet" are vague adjectives and should be avoided.

"Thing" is a word which can be applied universally. Again, it is a vague word. An elephant is a big "thing", a mouse is a small "thing", a car is a "thing", as is any noun you care to name. When you say "please pass me that "thing", what are you referring to? Do you mean please pass me that elephant? Be specific. Use an exact noun.

The phrase "fed up" is not good grammar and should be avoided. Nevertheless, it is widely used and generally with the incorrect preposition! If you use "fed up" it <u>must</u> be followed by "with". Never "of". "I am fed up <u>with</u> doing homework".NOT "I am fed up <u>of</u> doing homework".It would be preferable to use "tired of", "bored by" "exasperated with" instead of "fed up with".

Use the correct tense of verbs. It is correct to say "she said to me..." when reporting a conversation, because it has already taken place, that is, it is in the past, so we use the past tense. To say, when reporting a conversation "she says to me..." is wrong, because it was the wrong tense. You must never report a past event in the present tense. It is equally wrong, for the same reason, to say "He comes to my house, sits down at the table and eats all my dinner", when you are telling someone that this happened. The correct grammar is "He came to my house, sat down at the table and ate all my dinner".

Another example of bad grammar is the common use of the word "goes" when reporting speech. Not only the tense, but also the word itself is wrongly used. The word should be "say" not "go". Cars and engines "go". People say; ask, cry, whisper, shout, murmur, bellow, inquire, wonder, inform, insist, relate, repeat, exclaim, mutter, suggest and tell. They do NOT "go".

SHALL AND WILL

We use SHALL with "I" and "we" and WILL with "he", "she", "it" "you" and "they" to express the future.

There are occasions when we do say "I will" or "you shall" quite correctly, but in these cases we are expressing determination. For example:

a) I shall go to the cinema.
b) I will go to the cinema.

Sentence a) means that you intend going to the cinema at some future time. Sentence b) means that you are determined to go:

c) Matthew will go to bed.
d) Matthew shall go to bed.

Sentence c) means that Matthew will go to bed at some future hour. Sentence d) means that Matthew is to go, probably as a punishment.

Rewrite the following sentences inserting "shall" or "will" in the blank spaces:

I ________ be sixteen next Friday.
You may not like it but you ________ take your medicine.
I ________ not tolerate careless work from any pupil.
By this time next week, Tom ________ be on his way from Australia.
Daisy may be as stubborn as she likes but she ________ apologise.
You ________ certainly be interested in all you see at the exhibition.
Britons never, never, never ________ be slaves.
You ________ find the book on your desk.

LIE and LAY

The words "lie" and "lay" are often confused. Remember that there are two different verbs, a) the verb to LIE and b) the verb To LAY.

The verb TO LIE has two meanings in common use.

1) To rest or learn:

Present Tense lie	Past Tense lay
let sleeping dogs lie	Present tense
He lay on the couch	Past tense
The cat lies on the rug	Present tense
The cat lay on the rug	Past tense

2) To speak falsely:

Present tense lie	Past tense lied

The verb TO LAY has several meanings:

Present tense lay	Past tense laid

1) To produce eggs:

The hens lay eggs	Present tense
The hens laid eggs	Past tense

2) To place, set down, or apply:

he lays a fuse	Present tense
The master laid his papers down	Past tense
Jack has come to lay the table	Present tense

3) To cause (sea, wind, dust) to subside:

The rain comes to lay the dust	Present tense

SENTENCE CONSTRUCTION

We can construct a useful sentence in this way: " She did this and then she did that." But if we construct all our sentences in this way they will become monotonous and dull. To make our writing as lively and pleasing as possible we must give plenty of variety to their construction. Here is a list of some of the ways in which the construction of a sentence can be varied:

We finished washing up, and then went out.
We had finished washing up, so we went out.
As we had finished washing up we went out.
After washing up we went out.
Having washed up, we went out.
When the washing up was finished we went out.
We went out, for the washing up was finished.
We went out, having first washed up.
We went out, after washing up.
We went out, when the washing up was finished.

Now rewrite each of the following sentences in as many different ways as you can:

We sang loudly and kept up our spirits.
I shouted to my friends and led the way up the narrow sheep-track.
He punctured his tyre, so he mended it by the roadside.
You wish to obtain success, so you must work hard.
The children were robbed of their toys, so they were very upset.

Part 3

PUNCTUATION

PUNCTUATION

Punctuation marks are used to help the reader to understand what has been printed or written. This is explained more fully later in this section

THE FULL-STOP

THE FULL-STOP is placed at the end of a sentence.
The FULL-STOP marks the end of an address.
The FULL-STOP is used after shortened forms. For example:

Mr. (Mister)	St. (Street or Saint)	Rd. (Road)
Mrs. (Missis)	Ave. (Avenue)	Dr. (Doctor)
Miss. (Mistress)	3rd. (third)	Cres. (Crescent)

The FULL-STOP is used after single letters standing for whole words. It is also used after abbreviations. For example:

A.D.	(anno domini)	In the year of our Lord.
A.M.	(ante meridiem)	Before noon.
P.M.	(post meridiem)	After noon.
B.A.	(Bachelor of Arts)	
G.M.T.	(Greenwich mean time)	
B.B.C.	(British Broadcasting Corporation)	
U.S.A.	(United States of America)	
Anon.	(Anonymous)	
Mod. Con.	(Modern Convenience)	

Re-write the following inserting capital letters and full-stops in their correct place:

it is early when the milkman comes i can hear the clink of his cans when i peep from my bedroom window i can see his horse it is a friendly old horse his name is dobbin sometimes when i have been up early enough i have fed him best of all he likes carrots the milkman always gives him an apple he likes that too.

CAPITAL LETTERS are always used after a full stop, question mark, or exclamation mark.

Capital Letters are always used to begin the first of a series of spoken words.

The judge replied, "Bring in the prisoner."

Capital Letters begin the first word of each line of poetry.

"Twinkle, twinkle, little star,
How I wonder what you are."

Capital Letters are always used to begin Proper Nouns.

Capital Letters are always used for all the names of God and for pronouns which stand for such names:

The Lord His mercy dwell with Him

Re-write the following sentences inserting Capital Letters where necessary.

1) the floor is wood. it has a carpet upon it.
2) is he ready? not quite.
3) what a lovely day! yes, it is.
4) he asked "will you come?"
5) when jesus christ was four years old,
the angels brought him toys of gold.

6) jane and robert are going to france in july.
7) i will come to play after i finish my homework.

THE COMMA

The comma shows where a slight pause must be made when reading, as:

Having forgotten my umbrella, I borrowed a raincoat.

A Comma is also placed before spoken words, as:

He said, "Let me go home".

The Comma is used to separate words in a series as:

I have not money enough to buy shoes, flower-pots, buckles, boxes and everything.

(There is no comma between the final pair of words in the list since they are separated by "and".)

The comma is used to separate an introductory word or group of words from the main part of the sentence, as:

Luckily, the weather yesterday was mild.
The weather being fine, we went for a pic-nic.

The comma is used to cut off a word, or group of words, which interrupts the sense of the sentence, as:

He dipped his brush in the paint, and, after mopping his forehead, continued to paint the fence.
The prisoner, who had a shifty appearance, made a poor impression on the jury.
The tent, surprisingly, withstood the full fury of the gale.

Re-write the following sentences inserting commas where necessary:

1) Rob was an auburn-headed shambling awkward lad with an

uncommonly wide mouth very red cheeks a turned-up nose and certainly the most comical expression I ever saw!

2) Over the hill over the dale through bush and through river they sped on their way.
3) Having arrived late the pupil was asked to remain behind to explain his lateness.
4) The colours of the rainbow are red orange yellow green blue indigo and violet.
5) This year at school I am studying English Maths French German Geography History Music Art and Science.
6) Hardly had we seen the lightning when a tremendous peal of thunder crashed overhead.
7) The contents of an average boy's pockets usually include a knife string a few nails one or two pencils a conker a handkerchief and some sticky sweets.
8) Finally we offer this beautiful blue vase for sale.

Re-write the following passage inserting Capital Letters, full-stops and commas where necessary.

two hikers stopped at a cafe' for lunch the waiter brought them two soles one large and the other one tiny human nature being what it is neither wanted to serve the fish eventually however one of them was prevailed upon to do so he gave his friend the small one and kept the large one for himself.

When we speak to each other, we make certain pauses here and there and introduce various tones or inflections of the voice. These pauses and inflections give meanings to our words which the words by themselves would not indicate. We need to give the same meaning to written and printed words and to do this we employ PUNCTUATION. We use signs to represent pauses and these pause signs are known as the comma, the semi colon, the dash, the colon and the full-stop. We also use apostrophes, question marks, exclamation marks and inverted commas.

Take the word "yes". If you were very determined you would say it sharply and emphatically. When writing, you would need to use an exclamation mark and write "Yes!" If you were using "yes" in a questioning way, your voice would gradually rise and when writing you would need a question mark to indicate this, so you would write "Yes?"

The word punctuation comes from the Latin word "puncto" which means "a point"; the words punctuate, puncture and punctual all come from the same root-word. So we punctuate by means of points or stops.

It is important to punctuate very carefully as a misplaced or omitted stop alters the sense of the passage. The full-stop indicates the longest pause, and it usually marks the end of a sentence. Too many full-stops in a passage give short, jerky sentences. This can be avoided by using conjunctions to link sentences or by using Relative Pronouns or Adverbs to weave sentences together.

Too few full stops give rambling sentences; the sentences go on, and on, and on without those pauses you would naturally make if you were speaking. The comma indicates the shortest pause and should be used where a slight pause would be necessary if the passage were spoken.

THE SEMI-COLON

This sign is used for a pause where a comma would be of insufficient value and a full-stop would be too sudden a pause. It separates complete sentences that are closely related; a full-stop would interfere with the easy flow of the reading. The semi-colon can be very useful when a writer wishes to create a feeling of excitement. As:

The lane was dark; the bushes rustled; the wind whispered.

The Semi--colon separates contrasting statements:

She is very plump; I am thin.
I met Mrs Smith yesterday; tomorrow I shall visit her sister.

Re-write the following sentences inserting semi-colons where necessary.

I came I saw I conquered.
Every house was destroyed every family was homeless.
I hate cricket I love tennis.
I have decided to go back I shall not stay long.
Neither of us spoke we waited in silence to see what would happen.

THE COLON

The colon is used to indicate a decided pause. We use it before the opening of a quotation. As:

The minister began his sermon with these words: "Go ye into the world."

The colon is mainly used in the introduction of a series or list of things, a catalogue of events and so on, as:

The ingredients of Christmas pudding are these: flour, suet, dried fruit, peel, spice, eggs, almonds and brown sugar.

We make three types of cars:- the saloon, the tourer, and the sports model.

THE DASH

The dash is used with a colon as in the example above, that is, before the details of a list.

Please supply:- a hammer, nails, a saw and pliers.

The dash is used to make a definite pause for effect. As:

And yet - to pass along busy streets....

The dash is used in dialogues

I knew - I mean I thought I knew....

THE QUESTION-MARK

The question-mark is placed at the end of a sentence which asks a question, as:

"Where is my hat?"
"Who spoke to you?"

These are Direct questions.
After an Indirect question, we use a full-stop. For example:

"Is the child ill?" asked the nurse.	Direct question.
The nurse asked if the child was ill.	Indirect question.
"Which is the way to the cinema?" asked the lady.	Direct question.
The lady asked the way to the cinema.	Indirect question.

Note the position of the question-marks. They are placed inside the quotation marks or inverted commas. "?"

Show how wrong punctuation has given the following sentences the wrong meaning. Re-write them with the punctuation that will give them their intended meaning.

1) In came a soldier on his face, a fiery look on his feet, his sandals on his back, his armour shouting aloud his battle-cry.

2) What do you think I work for? Nothing and pay for the pleasure of it.

3) The customers I know, are important.

4) His eyes malevolent, little beads followed my slightest move.

Re-arrange the following sentences to make each one form a question:

Jack and Jill went up the hill.

She wore a new hat.
The train will arrive in a few minutes.
It will be late.

STATEMENTS AND QUESTIONS

STATEMENTS	QUESTIONS
Toothache is painful.	Is toothache painful?
John plays well.	Does John play well?
Sally can see the players.	Can Sally see the players?
Father has been gardening.	Has Father been gardening?

A STATEMENT is a sentence giving information, that is, it states something.
A QUESTION is a sentence asking for information.

From the above examples you will see that the question-form varies from its statement-form by:

A different arrangement of the words.
A change in the form of the verb.

In the question-form, the Auxiliary verb "does" has been introduced. The Auxiliaries "do" and "does" are often used in sentences which are questions:

Use "does" with singular subjects.
Use "do" with plural subjects.

A question is followed by a question-mark when a statement is spoken, the tone of the voice sometimes turns a statement into a question; in such cases, the statement is followed by a question-mark, thus: I expect you miss your brother? This statement really means: Do you miss your brother?

All the questions in our examples can be answered by the words "yes" or "no". If you answered each by the word "yes", this word takes the place of the corresponding statement. As:

Is toothache painful?	Yes. =	Toothache is painful.
Does John play well?	Yes. =	John does play well.

So the word "yes" is called a sentence-word, that is, it is a word used in place of a sentence. In the same way, "no" is a sentence-word.

There are other question-forms which cannot be answered by one of the sentence-words, as:

What did he say?
Who broke this pen?
When did he come?
Where is my knife?

Here the Pronouns "what", "who" and the Adverbs "when", "where" introduce the question-form.

Change these statements into questions:

The weather yesterday was mild.
The house stands by an old mill.
Your dog is very obedient.
The meeting was held in the town hall.
You can't find your hat.
He has some roses in his garden.

THE EXCLAMATION MARK

The Exclamation Mark is used after an exclamation expressing disbelief, sudden pleasure, pain, surprise, alarm or annoyance as:

What!	What fun!	Good boy!
Oh yes!	Poor man!	Hurrah!

The Exclamation Mark is placed after words which express an order as:

Halt!	Silence!	Be quiet!
Put your cap on!	Attention!	Sit up!

The Exclamation Mark is used after exclamations but NOT after statements or questions. Note the position of the Exclamation Mark. Like question-marks it is placed inside the inverted commas. "!"
Arrange each of the following sets of words firstly as an exclamation and secondly as a question. This will make 18 sentences in all. Use Exclamation Marks and Question Marks in the appropriate places.

Home like place no is there.
Lucky I am home.
Told be you won't.
You for news got I have.
Boy naughty a you are.
It found I have.
Good not this is.
You properly behave will.
Smack I you shall.

INTERJECTIONS

In order that we may give vent to our feelings, we often make little noises or exclamations like:

Oh! Ah! Eh! Ho! Hallo! Alas! Hurrah!

Such words are called Interjections, for this word means "thrown among" (from the Latin word Jacio- I throw). They are words thrown among other words, and they have no definite work in a sentence.

An interjection begins with a capital letter.

As an interjection expresses excitement or deep emotion, it is followed by an exclamation mark. (!)

Find the Interjections in the following sentences and say what the speaker means each one to express:

Hurrah! tomorrow is a holiday.
He is a horrible man; ugh!
Alas! he will see no more the light of the sun.
Oh! this is perfect summer weather.
Oh! must we really do such unpleasant work?
Oh! you are treading on my toe.
Hello! is anyone at home?
Pooh! any fool could do that.
Bah! am I to listen always to the snivellings of a fool?
Fie! my Lord, fie! a soldier and afraid?

Exclamatory remarks, or interjections, can be abused by over-use. It is the lazy speaker or writer who sprinkles his language with too many exclamations. He is trying to produce a lively effect but fails to, because he succeeds in producing only a false emphasis. If you wish to speak or write sincerely, you must be prepared to think out and express clearly what you do mean.

With what punctuation mark does each sentence end? Re-write the following sentences inserting the correct punctuation marks. (Full-stop, question-mark or exclamation mark).

This chef cooks well
Is the sun shining brightly
How fast she runs
Climb up that ladder
How hard Joe is working
Have you seen the pantomime
What an extraordinary play this is
A rolling stone gathers no moss
How time flies
I am wondering whether to take the right turning or the left

THE APOSTROPHE

The Apostrophe is a lifted comma used in two ways:

With a noun, to show possession as in:

The boy's cap	The child's toy

In a word, to show that a letter has been left out, as in:

Don't (do not)	What's (what is)

So we can say, more briefly, that

"An Apostrophe indicates omission or possession".

The use of the Apostrophe to indicate possession is confined mainly to living things. Otherwise we use "of." For example:

	The man's leg was injured.
BUT	The leg of the table was damaged.

There are, as always, many exceptions to this general rule and expressions like "The Sun's rays", "The Car's speed", "The aeroplane's flight" are common.

When a noun is singular we add -'s to the original word, thus

man - man's	boy - boy's

When a noun is plural and ends in "s" we add the apostrophe after the final "s" thus:

ladies - ladies'	uncles - uncles'

Proper names ending in "s" should add 's but sometimes we simply add the apostrophe alone, because the extra "s" would sound awkward.

For example:

Burns' poetry and Keats' poetry sounds better than
Burns's poetry and Keat's poetry

It is correct to write:
St. James's church
Charles's pencil etc.,

We write:

Queen's College, Oxford
Queens' College, Cambridge

because the college at Oxford was named after one queen, whereas the college at Cambridge was founded by two queens.

As the correct use of the apostrophe is quite difficult to learn we will look at this again with more examples.

Possession - Singular Nouns
The girl's hat - the hat of the girl.
The boy's ball - the ball of the boy.
The lady's umbrella - the umbrella of the lady (one lady).
The dog's kennel - the kennel of the dog.
The clown's nose - the nose of the clown.

One girl, one boy, one lady, one dog, one clown. All singular so we just add 's.

Possession - Plural Nouns
The boys' school - the school of the boys.
The girls' college - the college of the girls.
The ladies' compartment - the compartment of the ladies (many ladies).
The dogs' home - the home of the dogs.
The clowns' antics - the antics of the clowns.

Many boys, many girls, many ladies, many dogs, many clowns. All plural, but all already end in "s" so we just add the apostrophe.

BUT when the plural noun does NOT end in "s" we add the apostrophe and "s".

The men's team - the team of the men.
The children's toys - the toys of the children.
The people's choice - the choice of the people.
The women's movement - the movement of the women.
The gentlemen's club - the club of the gentlemen.

So we arrive at:

The doctor's bills - the bills of one doctor.
The doctors' bills - the bills of more than one doctor.
A week's notice - notice of one week.
Three weeks' notice - notice of three weeks.
The lady's hat - the hat of one lady.
The ladies' hats - the hats of more than one lady.

Omission

We use the apostrophe to show, or indicate, where a letter has been missed out , or omitted. Thus:

What's your name? - What is your name?
It's Jane. - It is Jane.
He's a bad boy. - He is a bad boy.
Who's there? - Who is there?
There's no smoke. - There is no smoke.
Can't - Cannot
Won't - Will not.
Don't - Do not.
Haven't - Have not.
Wouldn't - Would not.

Shouldn't	-	Should not.
Didn't	-	Did not.

Re-write the following, inserting the apostrophes in their correct places:

a dogs tail	childrens toys	a girls school
horses manes	the daisies head	birds beaks
ladies umbrellas	Daises petals	blind babies home
Peters wifes mother	kittens tails	the ladys hats

Re-write the following sentences inserting apostrophes where they have been omitted:

Whos knocking at the door?
Twas a famous victory.
I wont come until ten oclock.
Ill row you oer the ferry.
Weve Raleighs still for Raleighs part.

PARENTHESIS

Parenthesis is a word, clause or sentence inserted into a passage to which it is not grammatically essential. It can also be a word or clause inserted in a sentence which is grammatically complete without it.

Usually we use parenthesis for explanation or to confirm something or expand upon something. The Greek word parenthesis means "to put in beside". So within our sentences or passages we "put in beside" things we want to explain or expand upon and we do this by using either brackets, or dashes or commas thus:

The child must always feel that (no matter what happens) his parents are to be trusted.
The child must always feel that - no matter what happens - his parents are to be trusted.
The child must always feel that, no matter what happens, his parents are to be trusted.

Remember, when using Parenthesis, that if you use brackets, having opened them, you must always close them. You cannot have half a bracket! The same rule applies to the dash, when it is used for parenthesis. If you open a dash, you must close it. Likewise, when using commas for parenthesis use one at the beginning of whatever you wish to enclose, and another at the end. This use is not to be confused with the normal use of commas where we simply insert them when a short pause is needed.

This sounds more complicated than it really is, so to show how simple parenthesis is, here are some more examples:
Smith - the burley Constable - was promoted to Sergeant.
George Bernard Shaw, playwright, spoke next.
Shortly after dawn, Eric (the most alert member of our crew) sighted the rescue ship.
London, the capital of England, is a fascinating city.
He is wholly trustworthy and (I can assure you) honest as the day is long.

All these sentences are grammatically complete without parenthesis, but we have "put in beside" things which we wanted to explain (the capital of England) or confirm (I can assure you) or expand upon (the most alert member of our crew).

Rewrite the following sentences using <u>parenthesis</u>:

Kathy the new pupil proved to be an excellent gymnast.
Parliament the seat of the British government opened yesterday.
Some children playing in the road caused an accident.
The old pensioner bent double with rheumatism sat on the park bench.
The football match arranged for Saturday has been postponed.
The car which has only had one owner has already done high mileage.
The policeman who was injured whilst on duty receives a pension.
The new girl who is proving to be popular looked very smart.
I was I must admit extremely surprised.
After school since it was a very hot day they went swimming.
The material a light summery cotton was very attractive.
The house which has been for sale for months belongs to my friend.

INVERTED COMMAS

These are also known as speech marks or quotation marks. Whenever we need to record the actual words spoken by a person, we must use Inverted Commas (inverted meaning upside-down). Inverted Commas are placed before the first word actually spoken, and after the last word actually spoken.

Certain rules have to be observed when Inverted Commas are used:

a) Tom said, "My sister is now going to school."
b) "My sister is now going to school", Tom said.

a) The first word of the quotation begins with a capital letter.
b) A comma separates the quotation from the other words, because the actual sentence does not end in school, it ends in "said".

Every word enclosed by the Inverted Commas must be actually spoken by the speaker.

With very few exceptions, the punctuation mark (full stop, comma, exclamation mark or question mark) is placed between the last word spoken and the Inverted Commas, as:

"Hurrah!" shouted the crowd.
Chloe asked, "Are you going to netball?"

When a question is broken, two sets of Inverted Commas must be used:

"Be very careful", Mother said, "when you cross the road."

Note that no capital letter is needed for the first word of the second part of a broken quotation.

DIRECT and INDIRECT SPEECH

Sometimes a passage does not give the exact words used by a speaker. As:

Tom said that his sister was now going to school.

This sentence gives the same meaning as sentence a) but it does not give the exact words spoken by Tom.

When Inverted Commas are used and the passage gives the exact words spoken, that passage is said to be written in DIRECT SPEECH.

When no Inverted Commas are used and the passage gives the meaning of the words spoken without using the exact words uttered, the passage is said to be written in REPORTED or INDIRECT SPEECH.

When changing direct into indirect speech, care must be taken with the following points:

If the report is made in the past tense, then the verbs in the direct speech will have to be changed accordingly.

When the report is made by someone else, all the pronouns must be changed. For example:

John said, "I shall put away my books when I come home."
John said that he would put away his books when he came home.

If the speaker reported his own speech, the personal pronouns would not change.
As:

I said I would put away my books when I came home.

Words such as "today", "tomorrow", "this", "these", "here", "now", in direct speech change to "that day", "next day", "that", "those", "there", "then", in indirect speech.

Auxiliary verbs "shall" and "will" become "should" and "would".

When changing a passage from Direct to Indirect speech you will use the word "said". Do not overwork this word. Try to use other words such as:

exclaimed	shouted	replied	muttered
remarked	cried	answered	retorted
inquired	declared	asked	demanded

Here are some examples of how to change **Indirect** into **Direct** Speech:

The boy said that he was very sorry. (INDIRECT)
The boy said, "I am very sorry." (DIRECT)

(Note the changes in the Pronoun - **he** becomes **I**- and the verb - **was** becomes **am** - the omission of the word "that", and the addition of a comma).

The man asked where the picture was to be hung. (INDIRECT)
The man asked, "where shall I hang the picture?" (DIRECT)
Father asked where that man was. (INDIRECT)
Father asked, "where is this man?" (DIRECT)

The following sentences, from which all punctuation has been omitted, contain Direct Speech. Rewrite each sentence inserting all the necessary punctuation and Inverted Commas:

why are you teasing the cat sally asked her brother it is doing you no harm
there is no need said the speaker for anyone to go hungry there is plenty of food for all
you worked so hard last term lucys mother told her that your father has bought you a watch as a reward
i cannot understand said jack with a sigh where all my pocket-money goes
as soon as the whistle sounds announced the instructor all activity must cease

Rewrite the following sentences turning them from INDIRECT to DIRECT speech, the actual words of each speaker will be shown:

1) My brother said it was necessary for me to go.
2) The farmer told me that, having lost both his sons, he was going to sell the farm.
3) The fairy said that she would take me to fairyland.
4) Charlie asked me if I could keep a secret.
5) The master asked him why he had come and what his name was.
6) My father said he would take me with him to the concert.
7) The teacher told the boy not to be afraid.
8) Daisy replied that she could not play in the match the next day because shehad to help her mother.
9) The postman said that there were not enough stamps on the letter and that he wanted fifteen pence extra.
10) The butcher ordered the man out of the shop.

Rewrite the following passage turning it from DIRECT to INDIRECT or reported, speech. Do not use any exact words uttered, and do not use inverted commas:

"There are too many spiders about", said the fly. "No corner is safe from them; they squat in the grass and pounce on you. I've got an ache in my eye from trying to watch them. They are ugly, hungry people without manners or neighbourliness, terrible, terrible creatures".

"I have seen them", said the cow, "but they never do me any harm. Move up a little bit, please, I want to lick my nose: It's funny how itchy my nose gets" - the fly moved up a bit. "If", the cow continued, "you had stayed there, and if my tongue had hit you, I don't suppose you would ever have recovered."

Part 4

COMPREHENSION AND RECAPITULATION

CONTENTS

Page

A SHORT INTRODUCTION AND EXPLANATION

This section aims to encourage intelligent reading; that is, to improve upon the retention of facts, details, descriptions and the exact meaning of what is being read. To this end, there is, after each passage an exercise to test the understanding or comprehension of the passage just read, and to encourage the child to concentrate on the content of his reading-matter.

This is important, since it will help the child not only with his English, but with all his other school subjects. It can be said that if a child learns to read intelligently whilst still young, it will become a habit which will stay with him throughout his life and stand him in good stead.

Not for him the superficial "skimming-over" of written material, which can often result in vital facts being missed or instructions misunderstood. These misfortunes can, in turn, lead to disastrous consequences. There is a great deal of difference between reading, and reading intelligently.

In examinations, the test of ability in reading is confined mainly to Comprehension exercises since they provide training in careful and thoughtful reading.

The comprehension questions in this book are based mainly upon exactness of meaning, vocabulary, illustration of general statements and close examination of figures of speech. They are intended to sharpen the child's mind in the assimilation and critical consideration of what he reads.

A series of revision or recapitulation exercises in Grammar, figures of speech and punctuation appear after the comprehensions. These exercises are designed to reinforce the learning of the Grammar, figures of speech and punctuation which we have steadily worked through with examples and exercises in earlier sections of this book.

Practice and repetition are infallible tools for the learning process, and for this reason many exercises are frequently repeated (though all with different contents). If the child works carefully through these exercises he should have a sound understanding of the essence of English Grammar.

THE DISRUPTIVE PUPIL

Edwin Johnson, a class friend of his, had an annoying habit of giggling. Unfortunately for Alan it was infectious. Alan simply couldn't resist breaking into an uncontrollable bout of laughter whenever he caught Edwin's eye (which was quite often). Miss Matthews promptly placed Alan in the front row (to the grinning delight of his fellow pupils) and with a stern frown and a peremptory nod, relegated Edwin to the back of the class.

During a particularly boring part of the lesson, Alan looked over his shoulder and caught a glimpse of Edwin's face. Of course this upset the other members of the class and resulted in Alan (a very sorry Alan, by now) being called out to receive a stroke of the cane. But Alan noticed a little twinkle in Miss. Matthew's eye as she delivered the punishment and this helped him make up his mind not to slack - somehow he felt that she was on his side.

COMPREHENSION

1) Why does the writer say "unfortunately" for Alan?
2) Explain the meaning of the word "relegated" as it is used in the passage.
3) What does "peremptory" mean? You may use your dictionary.
4) How do we know that this is not set in the present time?
5) Using your own words, give the meaning of "delivered the punishment."
6) What does the phrase "to the grinning delight of his fellow pupils" mean?
7) Why did "this upset the other members of the class"? (paragraph two)
8) Do you think Miss Matthews was angry when she caned Alan? Give your answer in your own words.
9) Find four different conjunctions used in the passage.
10) Give one example of Metaphor used in the passage.
11) In the first paragraph, the author uses the adjective "uncontrollable". Say whether you think this is effective, and suggest a precise synonym for it.

12) Give the meaning (as used in the passage) of the word "infectious." Use your own word or words in your explanation.
13) Why was Edwin's habit of giggling "annoying"? (paragraph one)
14) Give one example of Parenthesis.
15) Who was the "disruptive pupil?"
16) Give the meaning of the word "disruptive". You may use your dictionary.
17) Name two verbs and two nouns from the passage. Write against each of them whether they are verbs or nouns.
18) Why did Miss. Matthews place Alan in the front row?
19) Name two adjectives and two adverbs from the passage. Write against each of them whether they are adjectives or adverbs.
20) "a class friend of his" - a class friend of whom? (Line one).

RECAPITULATION

1) Write the questions to which these are the answers:

Because it is too dark to read without it.
No, the rain has stopped, so I shall not carry it.
Five pounds of potatoes and two pounds of apples, please.
Thank you, but my mother is expecting me home for tea.
One teaspoonsful for each person and one for the pot.
At Seven o'clock, as I have to cook the breakfast.
No, I was too busy today, but I took him for a long walk yesterday.
Yes, we have a dog, five hens and a cat.
I have no brothers, but I have three sisters.
Because I do not enjoy strawberries without cream and sugar.

2) Write questions beginning:

who...	whose...	by which...
which...	for what...	where...
what...	in what...	when...
how...	how much...	why...

3) Give the correct single word for each of the following:

A boy who sings in a choir.
The smallest pig in a litter.
A lady who writes poetry.
A man who sells meat.
A small room for changing into swimwear.
A man who carries luggage at a railway station.
A man who fixes glass in window frames.
A man who drives an aeroplane.
A woman who cares for the sick in hospital.
The sound made by an elephant.

4) Rewrite the following sentences replacing the words "get" and "got" with a verb chosen from this list.

returned	buy	climbed	was obliged
surmount	became	received	arrived
bring	reach	catch	

If I get the drinks, will you get the food?
He was able to get over the difficulty.
The child got a fright.
She got back to her work as soon as possible.
The thieves got over the wall.
Can you get the apples, or are they too high up on the tree?
The procession got to the gate of the city.
Emma wrote a list of the things she wanted to get from the supermarket.
The animals got excited and broke down the barrier.
Sophie and I will get the nine o'clock train to London.

5) Write the following sentences inserting Colons where necessary:

Each boy attending the camp had to provide himself with the following articles knife fork spoon plate mug and sleeping-bag.
Youth is the time for adventure and romance old age is the time for retirement and peace.

The Royal Navy inspires confidence it has always been the nation's defence against a foreign invader.
Houses are badly kept cooking hardly exists no one bothers to keep a garden much less to make clothes.
I have sometimes seen women of seventy with huge bundles on thieir backs one old lady had a grown-up son at home who owned a horse.
Day and night the doctor and his wife were among the sick nursing feeding and tending them with all that skill and care could do.
It was past midnight when they entered the harbour since it was the last exericse in their programme the late hour did not matter.
He turned and called out "Hooked on, sir!" to the bridge and they were at rest, and his part in the day was over.
There was a small ripple of laughter from the men Lockhart wondered if Phillips had already drunk his beer.
Then he took a last look at the moorings and said "All right - that'll do", and followed his party down the ladder.

6) Rewrite the following sentences, filling the blank spaces with the correct Relative Pronouns:

This is the dog _______ bit me.
Is this the same book _______ you were reading?
This is the man_______ I visited yesterday.
Here is the boy _______ won the English prize.
The farmer _______ haystacks were burnt.
He knows the person _______ started the fire.
Clive sold the dogs _______ he bought from my brother.
Sophie was speaking to the lady _______ we told you about.
Look at the man _______ is selling newspapers.
Do you know the children _______ the master is praising?

7) Rewrite the following sentences inserting apostrophes where they have been omitted, then write the apostrophised words in full:

They say they dont like children. They dont get on with them.
He said, "All right - thatll do".
Its time for tea, weve cream cakes today!

Thats right, its my suitcase, its your bag.
Lets go out to play, the suns shining.
Havent you finished your homework yet?
Sorry, I didnt mean to keep you waiting.
I hadnt noticed the time.
Whos the new girl in class? Shes very pretty!
Wasnt it a pity? She couldnt join in with the other girls.

RECOLLECTIONS OF CHILDHOOD

We lived in a cottage on the Moor, and had a small front garden with no room to grow vegetables. As there were seven children to feed, my father rented two allotments, one for all types of fresh vegetables and a much larger plot on which corn was grown, so that we had our flour for baking. All the bread was made at home by my mother.

At the age of about six, my greatest pleasure was to be with Dad on the allotment; I rode down there in the wheelbarrow. The entrance was by a large field gate which I would jump out of the wheelbarrow to open and then close behind us.

The allotments were separated by a track through the centre, which allowed carts to enter to carry away the heavy crops such as potatoes, otherwise many wheelbarrow trips would have to be made. Before we started planting the potatoes my Dad had a load of manure carted and left at the bottom of our plot. It was very easy to get manure then as there were many horses in the village due to the many farms.

About three parts of the vegetable plot was used for potatoes. My Dad had two thin iron rods, made by Mr Gouldthrope at the Smithy, with a point at one end and a ring handle at the other, with a rope between them, which was the line or measure. He dug a trench and put manure into it, and I had a little shovel too, so that I could help. We spaced out the seed potatoes on the manure and then covered them with the soil from the second trench. The rest of the plot was planted up with all types of greens and other vegetables.

(Reprinted by permission of "The Melbourn Magazine")

COMPREHENSION

1) What is an allotment?
2) How many brothers and sisters did the writer have?
3) What was Mr Gouldthorpe's trade?
4) What does the writer mean (in the last line of the passage) by "all types of greens?" Name three types of "greens."

5) In paragraph two, the writer mentions her greatest pleasure. What was this?
6) Why was it necessary to have manure before the potato planting began?
7) Explain why the farms had so many horses.
8) The passage describes a time long ago. Give four reasons why we know this.
9) Why was it necessary to close the gate behind them? (paragraph two).
10) Which vegetables did the writer's father grow the most of?
11) Why did the writer's father rent two allotments?
12) What does the word "rented" mean in the first paragraph?
13) What was grown on the larger of the two plots?
14) How do you think the corn was harvested in those days before tractors and combine-harvesters?
15) How would the corn have been made into flour for baking the bread?
16) Why don't modern farmers use manure very often?
17) What do modern farmers use instead of manure?
18) In what way did the writer help her father?
19) In what way do you think "seed potatoes" differ from potatoes that we eat?
20) Describe what you think the line or measure (paragraph four) was used for, and how it was used.

RECAPITULATION

1) Write the following sentences filling in each blank space with the correct word.Write next to each sentence whether it is a Simile, Metaphor, or Proverb:

The poor hedgehog was as _______ as a doornail.
It never _______ but it pours.
The ballet dancer seemed as light as a _______.
They worked _______ in glove together.
Take care of the _______ and the pounds will take care of themselves.
The boxers were going for each other hammer and ______ .
There's no smoke without _______.

He threw himself heart and _______ into his work.
The child slept like a _______.
Many _______ make light work.

2) Give one word for the following:

A person's life-story written by himself.
A person's life-story written by someone else.
A man who shoes horses.
A building in which soldiers live.
A printed list of items at a concert.
A small hole in a tyre.
A track beside a river or canal.
The place in church from which the Sermon is preached.
A man who collects news for a newspaper.
A number of hounds.

3) Write the following sentences, underlining the pronoun in each one:

He sang a short song.
The people cheered him.
The chair was kept for her.
At school she was always good.
You should always pay your debts.
They stood in the doorway.
Tell them that story.
It stood on the desk.
Everybody knows that song.
Anybody with any sense wouldn't do that!

4) Rewrite the following sentences ending with a full-stop, question-mark or exclamation-mark:

There is no place like school
It was his left hand he burnt
Will you time me for the quarter-mile, please
Gather round, my hearties

Would you like another sandwich
His courage helped him enormously
Are you sure you know the way
Fifteen men on a dead man's chest
Primroses are Sophie's favourite flower
Justin married Rosslyn in August

5) Write the following sentences inserting semi-colons where necessary.

Discipline is essential without it an army becomes a mere mob.
The ruffian picked up a stone suddenly he threw it with all his might at a plate-glass window there was a resounding crash as the window was shattered next minute the ruffian was running down the street with a tray of jewellery in his hands.
The rain started at first it came as a few large drops then it settled into a drizzle the drizzle became a downpour finally it seemed as if the heavens had opened to release a deluge of water on the earth below.
A slight noise attracted my notice and looking to the floor I saw several enormous rats traversing it.
Scrooge is a miser his facial appearance pointed nose shrivelled cheek red eyes and frosty hair all suggest as much and his habits confirm it.

6) Find the verb which gives the exact meaning of each of the following:

go on one foot
go with very long steps
go like a soldier
go lamely as though hurt
go on one's knees
go stealithily
go slowly and quietly
go with extreme hurry
go as if walking in slippers
go showing annoyance with feet

7) Write the following sentences underlining every adjective:

There were two grey crows, perched upon the shredded thatch, and sheltering behind the stumpy stone chimney.
Costly, elegant or sumptuous clothes will give the wearer grace and elegance.
Heavy clouds of smoke and heaps of smouldering rubble.
The teacher, with a worried frown, sat correcting exercises.
The kind housewife gave the beggar a bowl of soup.

We gazed spellbound at the closed curtain as if blinded by an unnatural vision.
He lifted his trunk almost vertically, together with his age-worn, reddish-brown tusks, and dropped it gently and slowly in a disdainful half-circle.
My first impression was one of genuine, deep admiration.

UNDERSTANDING YOUR CHILD

A good deal of preparation is necessary to equip the first child to meet the momentous event of a new baby with equanimity and joy.

From his earliest days he should be trained to be as independent as possible. Every baby is entitled to a great deal of mothering. Before and after feeds, his mother should play with him and should devote herself to this entirely. But in between these times the baby should be encouraged to amuse himself and learn to be self-reliant. At an early stage he should be accustomed to meeting strangers and being left by his mother without any fuss. There are mothers who are flattered if their baby yells and refuses to be pacified whenever they go out of sight. They should, in fact, be ashamed of letting the child develop this "mother-fixation".

Then again, long before a new baby arrives, the child should be accustomed to seeing its mother nurse another baby. Every opportunity for seeing and playing with babies should be used for this purpose, so that the child is relaxed and used to the idea of his mother holding babies, and grows to like and accept them.

Finally, I do emphasise again that free discussion of the baby before its birth is necessary. Not only is this a valuable step in the sex-education of the child, which any mother would be foolish to neglect, but it gradually accustoms the child to the idea of another one sharing his mother's love. It must be a cruel shock for any child to be suddenly confronted with a baby, who, to all intents and purposes, has taken his place. No wonder that in some cases the older child attempts to injure the baby.

Again , the child, in talking about the baby, and seeing the preparations feels he is sharing something with his mother, and this in itself will be satisfying and make him feel that he is of real importance to his mother.

When all these precautions have been taken, the stage is well set for the play to begin, but there still remains for it to be really well played.

(From "Understanding Your Child" by Dr. Winifred De Kok)

COMPREHENSION (A difficult one)

1) What does the author mean by "mother-fixation"? (paragraph two)
2) Do you agree or disagree with the author's views? Explain your point of view.
3) Describe, in your own words, the meaning of "mothering." (paragraph two)
4) Put into your own words the phrase "grows to like and accept."
5) Explain in you own words the meaning of "to be suddenly confronted."
6) Explain the meaning of the phrase "to all intents and purposes" then, keeping the sense of the sentence, replace it with a phrase of your own.
7) Find an example of a metaphor in the passage.
8) Explain what you understand the author to mean by "there still remains for it to be really well played."
9) Give one example of parenthesis taken from the passage.
10) In the first sentence the author uses the word "momentous." Why do you think she chose this particular word? Do you think it is effective?
11) Using your dictionary, find the meaning of "equanimity."
12) Explain the meaing now, of "equanimity and joy" as used in the first sentence of the passage. Keeping the sense of the sentence replace these words with your own.
13) What is the meaning of the phrase "devote herself to this entirely"? (paragraph two). Why is the adverb "entirely" important to this phrase?
14) The author uses the word "accustom" three times in the passage. Suggest two synonyms which she might have used instead.
15) From the passage give three ways in which the author suggests that a young child should be introduced to the idea of a new baby's arrival.
16) Using your dictionary explain the meaning of "precaution."
17) How does the author suggest that a baby should be trained to be "as independant as possible"?
18) What do you understand the phrase "self-reliant" to mean?
19) What is the meaning of the word "flattered"? Use your dictionary.
20) Rewrite "foolish to neglect" in your own words.

RECAPITULATION

1) Give a single Noun for each of the following:

A song sung by two people.
A group of people who sail a ship.
A man who cares for your teeth.
A group of people playing cricket.
A number of wolves.
A fast train.
A building where cars are kept.
A man who mends pots and pans.
The young of a badger.
The wooden edging round a doorway.

2) Add Prefixes to the following words to make Antonyms:

pleasant	tidy	polite	visible
able	possible	appear	usual
necessary	pure	fasten	honest

3) Write the following sentences ending with a full-stop, question-mark or exclamation-mark.

What a mess that looks.
Have you seen this mess.
I will not put up with this mess.
Where is my book.
Here is your book.
Give that to me.
What a lovely day it is.
Please, put the cat out.
Why doesn't she come.
I really don't have time for this.

4) Write the following sentences inserting the correct Adverbs in the blank spaces:

The sun shone ________ as we set off on holiday.
The ________ woman fed the starving stray kitten.
Put the parcel ________ then take off your coat.
She strolled ________ to the shops.
They ________ left the table and went into another room.
He wrote ________ in his new book.
________ the bucket was emptied.
There is ________ a flag at the masthead.
You should spell ________ or your meaning may become confused.
________ followed the procession.

5) Rewrite the following, inserting Apostrophes in their correct places:

The wolfs club
The thieves den
The oxens yoke
Mr Smiths rooms
A mans job

Their dogs tails
My childrens toys
The ladys car
Mr Joness rooms
A boys bicycle

6) Rewrite the following sentences and underline the Prepositions:

His coat is similar to mine, but his hat is different from mine.
Though similar in looks, the brothers differ from each other in temperament.
If you are too strict, your children will rebel against your rules.
She is a clever girl, accomplished in many things.
It is unfair for Matthew to be compared with Harry.
They strolled down the leafy avenue.
You failed your exams through laziness.
Two waiters shared the tip between themselves.
Down the road stalked the black cat.
Do not fall over the edge of the cliff.

7) These Proverbs have become "mixed". Rewrite them correctly:

A bird in the hand is worth two in one basket.

All work and no play will look after themselves.
Save the pence and the pounds will make Jack a dull boy.
Do not put all your eggs in the bush.
Waste not, there's a way.
Two wrongs are soon parted.
Where there's a will want not.
A fool and his money do not make a right.
While the cat's away, spoil the child.
Spare the rod and the mice will play.

CHRISTOPHER COLUMBUS

Today it is possible to cross the Atlantic by air in a few hours, but for Christopher Columbus, who first discovered the New World, it meant many weeks of uncomfortable and dangerous travel. Columbus was born in the Italian port of Genoa about 1450 and, after working at his father's trade of weaver, he went to sea at the age of fourteen. After many adventures he settled in Lisbon, the capital of Portugal, where he became a map-maker. He was soon convinced that such eastern countries as India could be reached by sailing westwards. He appealed in vain to the King of Portugal for funds to prove this theory, but eventually Queen Isabella of Spain furnished him with a small fleet and, on 3rd August, 1492, Columbus and his mariners set sail. The SANTA MARIA, the ship in which Columbus sailed as Admiral, was only ninety feet in length, and the other two vessels, the PINTA and the NINA, were even smaller. On 12th October, 1492, after a most difficult voyage, during which Columbus had to suppress mutiny among his crew, land was sighted.

Columbus believed that he had reached the continent of Asia, but we now know that he landed on one of the islands off the American continent, which, because of his error, are still known as the West Indies.

"Christopher Columbus" By J. H. Duffy and H. Martin

(reprinted by permission of Robert Gibson and Sons, Glasgow, Ltd)

COMPREHENSION

1) Give another name for "the New World".
2) Which two words show that Columbus' voyage was not an easy one?
3) Give two examples of parenthesis from the passage.
4) What nationality was Christopher Columbus?
5) How do we know that his appeal for funds to the King of Portugal was unsuccessful?
6) Which word tells us that Columbus continued trying to raise funds for his voyage?

7) Queen Isabella "furnished" him with a small fleet. Give another word (of your own) for "furnished".
8) How many ships did the "small fleet" consist of?
9) Columbus had to "suppress mutiny". Explain the meaning of this in your own words.
10) "Because of his error". Rewrite this in your own words, keeping the sense of the sentence.
11) Before Columbus sailed for the New World, he had worked in how many other occupations? What were those occupations?
12) In the passage, find and write down, ten proper nouns.
13) Columbus went to sea at the age of fourteen. Which phrase tells us that this was not a dull time for him?
14) How long did the voyage to the "New World" take?
15) Columbus and his "mariners". Give another word for "mariner". You may use your dictionary.
16) In describing two of the ships, the adjective "smaller" is used. Is this adjective positive, comparative, or superlative in degree?
17) From the passage, find and write down five prepositions.
18) From the passage, find and write down ten verbs.
19) Write down as many adjectives as you can find in the passage.
20) What was the occupation of Christopher Columbus' father?

RECAPITULATION

1) Rewrite the following sentences replacing the gaps with Antonyms for the words in italics:

Below the ground are the roots, ________ the ground are the flowers.
Seeds grow *quickly*, but trees grow ________.
When you climb a tree, always look ________, never look *down*.
The flower was yellow *inside* and blue ________.
The bees hummed ________, the dogs barked *loudly*.
The dwarf spoke *roughly*, the farmer answered ________.

2) Rewrite the following sentences inserting all capital letters,

punctuation and inverted commas:

how fat you are said the wolf i wish i could be the same
i work for my master replied the dog
i spend all night hunting said the wolf you never hunt at all
as well as my food i also have a warm kennel said the dog
ah my friend said he i shall not come with you
come with me said the dog i will find you good home
why is the hair on your neck worn away asked the wolf
oh said the dog carelessly that is the mark made by my collar
what work do you do asked the wolf
i guard the house at night answered the dog

3) Write out the following sentences underlining each Adverb:

He dressed himself carefully in his best clothes.
He walked briskly on.
The bridge had been entirely blown away.
He thought regretfully of his lost feast.
He turned sadly home again.
He walked slowly along looking for the ditch in which he had thrown the pears.
The sun shines brightly on all good people.
The birds sing happily in the woods.
The doctor spoke comfortingly to the sick child.
He carried the eggs carefully back to the kitchen.

4) Rewrite the following sentences in the Plural form, making the other necessary alterations agree with the Plural Nouns and Pronouns:

The horse was well taught.
He would stand by himself.
The man is wiser than the donkey.
This car is called a chariot.
He mowed down his enemy.
A scythe was fastened to the wheel.
The man leaped out and dealt a blow.

What does the lady wear round her neck?
The brother had shown much courage.
The lioness was crouching.

5) Give the <u>Prepositions</u> in the following sentences, and say which two words they relate:

To whom are you speaking?
He got off the train.
For us there is little hope.
You must apologise to the master.
He is an authority on ants and moths.
He is very proud of his son's success.
The cat jumped through the window.
Will you come with me to the dentist?
You cannot see beyond the horizon.

6) Give one word for each of the following:

A man who writes plays.
The capital of England.
Someone who leaves his own country.
A number of lions.
Eleven men playing rugby.
A man who discovers things by conducting experiments.
A period of ten years.
A group of people playing brass instruments.
A book which gives the meanings of words.
A man who sells fruit and vegetables.

7) Rewrite the following sentences inserting either "teach" or "learn" in each of the gaps, adding -s or -es to the verb when necessary:

The master ________, the boys.
When we ________ our lessons well, we receive good marks.
Let me ________ you how to sew.
The master takes pains to ________ Harry, but Harry is very slow to

________.

We will ask Mr Bolton if he ________ his boys the same lessons that we________.

You really must ________ to write neatly.

I cannot ________ you another thing unless you concentrate.

If you really want to ________, I will ________you.

TALES FROM THE ANIMAL HOSPITAL

Meanwhile candy's plight had been shown on live television and the phones erupted with people wanting to know the outcome, which was far from certain as Jeremy set about repairing her injuries. The operation took several hours, with constant filming, and was eventually completed at about 10,30 p.m. Four metal pins had been inserted in Candy's legs and, heavily sedated and full of painkiller, she was handed over to the nurses who would take care of her through the night. The resilience of animals, particularly the young never ceases to amaze me: the next day on my ward rounds Candy was purring and wanting food.

Ten million people witnessed our fight to save Candy and it certainly concentrated the minds of those who had indoor cats. Over the next three months we had only two or three more cases of high-rise syndrome - as the Americans call it. I reckon we prevented at least eighty cats in the London area from suffering a similar fate and goodness knows how many in the country as a whole. But the next summer we saw an increasing number of cases: the public's memory is short. One injured cat had been in the flat only two hours after arriving from the pet-shop. This is part of our job, a never-ending journey of education, but the power of television to do good is awe-inspiring. We need these programmes all year round.

From "Tales from The Animal Hospital"
by David Grant

COMPREHENSION

1) What kind of animal is Candy? Give one word from the passage which tells us.
2) What happened to Candy? How did the accident happen?
3) Explain what is meant by "Candy's plight".
4) The phones "erupted...". Say why this word is so effective and give your own word which you consider to be as effective.
5) What does the author mean by "high-rise syndrome". Who uses this phrase?

6) What reason does the author give for concluding that "the public's memory is short"?
7) Explain in your own words "a never-ending journey of education".
8) Why does the author feel that the television programmes are needed "all year round"?
9) What does the author consider to be part of the job of the R.S.P.C.A.?
10) Explain, in your own words, the meaning of "the resilience of animals."
11) Give an example, from the passage, of parenthesis.
12) How did the R.S.P.C. A. prevent "at least eighty cats" from having accidents like Candy's?
13) In what way did the fight to save Candy concentrate the minds of those who had indoor cats?
14) Give three adjectives used in the passage.
15) Give five personal pronouns used in the passage.
16) How long did it take to perform Candy's operation?
17) Give one phrase from the passage which informs us that Candy may not have survived.
18) Give three examples used in the passage of the use of apostrophe indicating possession. (Two words in each example).
19) How many people watched the television programme?
20) Which sentence in the passage tells us that the author is constantly surprised by the ability of animals to recover?

RECAPITULATION

1) The word "abstract" means "drawn away from", and so an Abstract Noun indicates a quality or feeling drawn away from the person or thing which possesses it. Such words as truth, whiteness, length, toothache are abstract nouns. Abstract nouns are usually derived from other words as:

strong - strength kind - kindness

Turn the following words into Abstract Nouns:

please	quick	good	bitter
free	just	king	cruel
long	wide	thrive	fool

2) Form a Verb (doing word) from each of these adjectives:

strong	fat	large	dear
weak	soft	feeble	moist
dark	glad	bitter	bold
clean	civil	fast	pure
human	rich	long	furious

3) Use one word to describe the following:

A place where stones are dug.
To make a noise like a horse.
To cut short, especially a word.
A person's life-story written by someone else.
A building where monks live.
Someone who finds out about foreign countries.
A man who drives and takes care of someone else's car.
A man who makes an entirely new machine.
A man who steers a ship in or out of a port.
A number of deer.

4) Insert the Apostrophe in the correct place in the following:

Four weeks time.
The babys pram.
A midsummer nights dream.
He is a neer-do well.
A weeks time.

Youre very lucky!
Were coming soon.
Six girls pets.
The ladies meeting.
The mens games.

5) Each of the underlined words in the following sentences is a Noun, Adjective, Verb, Adverb or Preposition. Say which part of speech each word is:

Give me a drink of water, please.
In the yard, there was a man.
The car stopped at the village inn.
He was the only person left in the room.
Do not be cross with me.
The children were running in and out.
Cross that sum out, it is wrong.
Late pupils will be given detention.
If you will only try you will succeed.
He came to my house late last night.

6) These Proverbs have become mixed, rewrite them correctly:

Too many cooks make light work.
Birds of a feather before they are hatched.
Speech is silver that glitters.
A stitch in time gathers no moss.
If at first you don't succeed, flock together.
All is not gold, silence is golden.
Don't count your chickens, try again.
Many hands spoil the broth.
A rolling stone saves nine.

7) Pair off the words in the left-hand column with their Synonyms in the right. Remember that only words that are the same part of speech can

be Synonyms: "Astonishment" and "Amaze" are not Synonyms, because one is a noun and the other a verb:

amaze	dingy
dreary	astonish
amazement	infantile
valid	explore
illegal	astonishment
puerile	illicit
rebuke	reprimand
unerring	exploration
reconnoitre	legal
reconnaissance	infallible

You may use your dictionary to help you.

TOBY TO THE RESCUE

Thursday was another hot and sunny day. Mrs. Brown was busy inside the cool, shady kitchen when the commotion began. Toby was barking frantically and rather more loudly than usual: there were other noises too, which sent an anxious Mrs. Brown scurrying into the garden.

Toby was growling fiercely and ominously and his barks woke the white doves from their sunbathed sleep beneath the apple tree and startled them into flight, their wings beating in unison as they climbed high into the perfect, cloudless sky.

Mrs. Brown hurried to Toby, who was planted solidly in front of the hen-run. His hackles were raised and his strong, white teeth threatened with each bark. Prudence was very frightened or very cross, for she had fluffed out all her feathers to make herself appear much bigger than she really was. She was also clucking and cackling noisily whilst making jerky little movements with her head and neck.

Mrs. Brown thought this was strange, since Prudence wasn't usually frightened by Toby, and whilst they were not precisely friends, they were, in general, peacefully tolerant of each other.

As Mrs. Brown reached Toby she saw the cause of all the panic!

A large ginger cat had entered the garden and prowling along the old brick path had evidently seen that the little door to the hen-run, normally safely fastened, was today wide open. It had been opened that morning to let Prudence have an unaccustomed wander around the garden. Prudence had timidly ventured out, scratching and pecking behind the water butt and underneath the currant bush and had even roamed as far as the dove-cote! Perhaps she had felt vulnerable in the garden's big world, or perhaps she preferred the shade of her run, whatever the reason, she had returned to her familiar home. But the door was still open.

The nimble ginger cat had seized his opportunity and was inside in a flash, crouching quietly, preparing to pounce, when Toby saw him and tried to frighten him off with growls and snarls and barks. Although Toby was trying to save Prudence, by standing so staunchly in front of the door, he had effectively blocked the cat's escape route. The cat, a hair-on-end creature of claws, arched back and erect tail, spat, hissed and growled: Toby barked furiously: Prudence clucked and cackled....

Mrs. Brown called :"Toby, come!". He came. The cat escaped through the little door way, up and over the fence.

Prudence held her ground, but continued complaining and fussing long after it was necessary.

COMPREHENSION

1) In what season do you think the story is set? Give two reasons for your answer.
2) What kind of animal is Prudence?
3) Describe, in your own words, what the writer means by "peacefully tolerant".
4) Why might Prudence feel "vulnerable" in the garden?
5) In your own words, give the meaning of "seized his opportunity".
6) In paragraph seven, the writer uses the adverb "staunchly". State why you think this particular adverb was chosen, and suggest a suitable alternative.
7) Explain what is meant by "Prudence held her ground".
8) In paragraph one, why does the writer refer to an "anxious" Mrs Brown?
9) Why might Prudence have "preferred the shade of her run"?
10) We are told in the first paragraph, "there were other noises, too" which sent Mrs Brown into the Garden. Name three of these noises.
11) What was the cat's escape-route?
12) How did Toby rescue Prudence?
13) Describe Toby's appearance when Mrs Brown arrived at the hen-run.
14) Why did Prudence appear to be "very frightened or very cross"?
15) Give two adverbs from paragraph three.
16) Give five adjectives from the first paragraph.
17) Give one example of idiom from paragraph five.
18) Keeping the sense of the sentence, rewrite "long after it was necessary" in your own words.
19) Find one metaphorical phrase in paragraph three.
20) What was the "cause of all the panic"?

RECAPITULATION

1) Write an Antonym for each of the following, and show that you understand its meaning by using it in a sentence of your own: (A dictionary will help you).

stern barren scanty resistless

2) State which of the following sentences are Metaphors, Similes or Proverbs:

The twins were as alike as two peas in a pod.
It is good to save for a rainy day.
Mary was engulfed in a sea of misery.
Two wrongs do not make a right.
The invaders swept through the country like a tornado.
Do not count your chickens before they are hatched.
Well begun is half done.
The father was chilly December; the Mother sunny June.
A coward is like ice that melts before a fire.
The chain-saw cut through the log like a knife through butter.
He ruled the country with an iron hand in a velvet glove.
He is the apple of his father's eye.
The investment turned out to be a goldmine.

3) Rewrite the following, inserting Capital Letters, Full-stops, and Commas where necessary:

many spiders go to great trouble to trap their particular prey twice a day they weave on bushes ferns or between branches of trees huge webs which are placed in such positions that they catch insects flying through the air

4) Give one word for each of the following:

A group of people gathered in church.
Fruit eaten at the end of a meal.
A private path leading to a house.

A place where films are made.
A bicycle made for two people.
A man who shovels coal into a furnace.
The part of the leg above the knee.
A water-filled ditch around a building.
A house on wheels.
A building where books are kept.

5) Using a dictionary, explain the difference in meaning between:

illegal	and	illicit
unsocial	and	anti-social
breech	and	breach
colonel	and	kernal
vein	and	vain
affect	and	effect

6) Write out each of the following Idioms in a separate sentence of your own to show that you understand its meaning:

A white elephant.
A wild-goose chase.
Cutting off his nose to spite his face.
To strike while the iron is hot.
To take the bull by the horns.
By all accounts.
To set your teeth on edge.
A flash in the pan.
To go from bad to worse.
Hobson's Choice.

7) Join the following sets of sentences into single sentences using Conjunctions:

Luke is fond of games. Jack prefers to read.
Zoe never eats sweets. She never eats sweet cakes.
Matthew lit the fire. Simon peeled the potatoes.
The boys went swimming. It was a very hot day.
School closed early. The pupils went home.
Tom arrived. Sam was just leaving.
Sophie shared all her toys. She's a very generous girl.
I have no pocket-money to give you. You have earned it this week.

The teacher was very angry. She did not give the class a detention.
I do not like fishing. I will come if you insist.

ABOUT MARY

There was once an orphan girl, far away in a little village on the edge of the moors. She lived in a hovel thatched with reeds, and this was the poorest and the last of all the houses, and stood quite by itself among brooms and heathers by the wayside.

From the doorway the girl could look across the wild stretches of moorland; and that was pleasant enough on a Summer day, for then the air is clear and golden, and the moor is purple with the bloom of heather and there are red and yellow patches of bracken, and here and there a Rowan tree grows among the big grey boulders with clusters of reddening berries. But at night, and especially a winter night, the darkness was so wide and so lonely that it was hard not to feel afraid sometimes. The wind, when it blew in the dark, was full of strange and mournful voices; and when there was no wind, Mary could hear the cries and calls of the wild creatures on the moor.

Mary was fourteen when she lost her father. He was a rough, idle, good-for-nothing, and one stormy night on his way home from the tavern he went astray and was found dead in the snow. Her mother had died when she was so small a child that Mary could scarcely remember her face. So it happened that she was left alone in the world, and all she possessed was a dog, some fowls, and her mother's spinning wheel.

But she was a bright, cheerful, courageous child, and soon she got from the people of the village sufficient work to keep her wheel always busy, for no-one could look into her face without liking her. People often wondered how so rude and worthless a fellow could have had such a child; She was as sweet and unexpected as the white flowers on the bare and rugged branches of the blackthorn..

Her hens laid well, and she sold all the eggs she could spare; and her dog, which had been trained in all sorts of cunning by her father, often brought her from the moors some wild thing in fur or feathers which Mary thought there was no harm in cooking.

Though she was all alone in the world, and had no girl of her own age to make friends with, she was happy and contented, for she was busy from morning till night.

COMPREHENSION

1) Find the sentence in paragraph two which contains nine adjectives.
2) How did Mary come to be alone in the world?
3) Name all the things that Mary possessed.
4) In what ways is a moor (a) like a meadow, (b) unlike a meadow?
5) From the passage, find the simile which describes Mary.
6) Mary's hovel stood "quite by itself". Using your own words replace this phrase.
7) What colour is the flower of the heather?
8) Give the seven adjectives which describe Mary.
9) Using the five adjectives from the passage, describe Mary's father.
10) Why was it hard for Mary "not to feel afraid sometimes"?
11) Using words from the passage as clues, say why we know the story is from a long time ago.
12) How did Mary manage to live?
13) What wild creatures in fur or feathers live on moors?
14) What is a spinning-wheel used for?
15) Why did Mary think there was no harm in cooking the creatures her dog brought?
16) How old was Mary when her father died?
17) What could Mary see from her doorway? Answer in two sentences.
18) Make four sentences telling how Mary spent her time each day.
19) Give an example of metaphor from the passage.
20) How do you think Mary's father died?

RECAPITULATION

1) Rewrite the following sentences, inserting the necessary <u>Punctuation</u> and <u>Inverted Commas</u>:

tom sat down stretched his legs removed his cap and began to read
the tramp was old wet weary and hungry
where do you get it i said i make it myself said the old man from the honey

which my bees make have you many bees i enquired.

2) The noun "Goodness" may be formed from the adjective "Good". Form <u>Abstract Nouns</u> from the following adjectives:

happy warm gay innocent true wise

3) Rewrite the following sentences, <u>using Inverted Commas</u>, turning them from indirect to <u>direct speech</u>:

The waiter announced that dinner was served.
We enquired at the station whether the bag had been found.
I asked him if he could tell us the way to the cinema.
He replied that it was several miles to the nearest railway station, but that a bus would soon be passing which would take us there.
The lady asked me the way to the post office.
I told her to take the second turning on the right.
Where are you going I asked.
The boy's reply was that he had lost his way.
The day is fine said mother so we will go.

4) Rewrite the following sentences, and <u>without</u> using Inverted Commas, turn them from direct to <u>indirect speech</u>:

"I have only fifteen pence in my pocket," said the boy.
"Slip out by the window," whispered Jack to Charlie.
The chief replied, "Kill me, rather than put me in prison."
"Must I go through the wood?" Sally asked. "It is the only way to the cave," replied the old lady, "but keep to the path, and you will be safe".
"Let me see you safely home." I begged.
"Oh! I have twisted my ankle!" she cried out.
"Why, "I asked the old lady" do you always do your washing on Mondays?"
He said, "Let me go home".
The teacher said, "You have all been given a holiday."

5) Use one word to describe the following:

A place in which to keep an aeroplane.
A shallow crossing over a river.
A large van for removing furniture.
An imaginary sight seen by a traveller in the desert.
A young swan.
A place where a very large volume of water is stored.
A group of people with the same surname living together in Scotland.
A fertile place in the desert.
A place where objects of historical and artistic interest are exhibited.
A group of stars.

6) The following is a mixed list of masculine and feminine nouns. List the masculine nouns then pair them with their feminine counterpart:

traitor	stag	duck	peahen
colt	peacock	gander	filly
drake	doe	ram	buck
goose	witch	traitoress	hind
ewe	heifer	bullock	wizard

7) In each of the following sentences there is one preposition. Write down the preposition and the two words it relates.

We rushed down the hill.
Heavy seas drove against the cliff.
Mist hid the path across the marsh.
The invalid on the settee groaned horribly.
The child behind him suddenly screamed.
The stranger gazed with suspicion.
His knife and fork fell noisily to the floor.
The cat climbed down the tree.
They ran for dear life.
We are always at your service.

HENRY I

Instead of having various great law-courts in London to decide cases, Henry I had only one court, called the King's Court.. The money coming from taxes was paid into the King's Court. Gradually, the officials who received the money, and knew how to keep count of it, came to form a separate court. This was called the Exchequer, from the chequered or checked table-cloth on which the money was placed in rows.

Henry I was a rich king, and was thought to have even more money than he needed. His subjects complained bitterly of the heavy taxes that he raised. He spent too much of these taxes on wars abroad, but he was careful to keep England at peace. There was no war in England for thirty years.

Everywhere the people praised "the good peace that the King made." Indeed they seemed to admire him for the rough justice he dispensed - such as having more than forty thieves hanged in one day from a great Oak tree. He was also very severe with those who made false coins, ordering their hands to be cut off. The idea was to make people afraid, or unable, to offend again.

Henry was a very active man, much given to travelling. In his latter years he spent most of his time in Normandy. But whilst he was in England, he visited all parts of it, even towns which had probably never seen a King of England before, such as Carlisle, Durham, and Norwich.

It seems that he really wished to see for himself that justice was done all over England. He sent his judges, who were officers of the King's court to every county in England.

The King's judges now sat in the Shire Court, and so they formed a link between the local courts of the hundred and the shire, and the Great Court of the King. At first, the judges had only been sent to receive the taxes, but in time they came to decide law cases as well.

Henry's forest laws were cruel, but he kept all the forests for himself, and his nobles were not allowed to hunt, and so did not oppress their poorer neighbours in the name of sport. In fact, Henry's great virtue was that, although he was something of a tyrant himself, he would allow nobody else to be one. And it was better to have one tyrant than to have a great number scattered all over the country. This was why the people forgave his heavy taxes and frequent wars abroad.

Henry I died in Normandy, in 1135, after a long reign of thirty-five years.

From "The Normans and Plantagenets" by J. Ewing

COMPREHENSION

1) What were the chief points which marked the reign of Henry I?
2) How did Henry pay for the wars abroad?
3) How did Henry improve the system of justice in England?
4) How long did peace last in England, under Henry?
5) From what do we get the word "Exchequer"?
6) Give an example of direct speech from the passage.
7) Two sentences in the passage start with conjunctions. Find these sentences and write down the first six words of each one.
8) Using your own words, give the meaning of "much given to travelling".
9) What other position did Henry's judges hold?
10) Give one word for someone who makes false coins or notes.
11) What happened to people who made false coins?
12) Which towns "had probably never seen a King of England before"?
13) What was Henry's great virtue, according to the author?
14) What was the reason for the severe punishments given to offenders?
15) The author mentions "the local courts of the hundred and the shire." What was a "hundred"? You may use your dictionary.
16) What was the original reason for the judges being sent to the shire court?
17) From the passage, give one example of parenthesis.
18) In your own words, give the meaning of "rough justice".
19) From the passage, give two adverbs of manner.
20) How does the author describe Henry's forest laws?

RECAPITULATION

1) Give one word for each of the following:

A tall building of many storeys.
A large piece of country where nothing grows.
A piece of wood used to keep a broken limb in place.
A vessel which carries goods on a canal.
The wooden weapon used by a policeman.
The goods carried by a ship.
A hundred years.
A man who minds sheep.
A book which gives addresses or telephone numbers.
A man who serves in a restaurant.

2) Rewrite the following sentences inserting the missing Apostrophes:

The boys book was found in the girls playground.
Each of the ladies carried a ladys handbag.
The mans hat attracted the childrens attention.
The owner gave three weeks notice.
Many ships passengers visited the island.
The heroes gathered at the heros memorial.

3) Rewrite the following sentences underlining each Adverb:

Our visitors did not come.
The patient had no pain, and slept peacefully.
He went very cheerfully to school.
Kick the ball over there! No, I want to kick it randomly.
She continued merrily on her way.
I pay my milk bill weekly.
You have done the work quietly and beautifully.
He attended his lessons regularly and punctually.
She spoke more sorrowfully than angrily.
The mission was completed successfully.

4) Use the following pairs of Homophones in sentences so that the differences in meaning are made clear:

envelop, envelope	advise, advice	story, storey
stationery, stationary	practice, practise	mantel, mantle

5) Choose, from the following list, the appropriate Verb, expressing sound, to complete each of the sentences.

brays	trumpets	whinnies	caws
gobbles	caterwauls	roars	grunts
howls	gaggles	croaks	bleats

The donkey _ _ _ _
The horse _ _ _ _
The rook _ _ _ _
The pig _ _ _ _
The sheep _ _ _ _
The lion _ _ _ _
The frog _ _ _ _
The cat _ _ _ _
The goose _ _ _ _
The elephant _ _ _ _
The turkey _ _ _ _
The wolf _ _ _ _

6) Using your dictionary, notice the different shades of meaning and use of the following Synonyms, and then use each one to fill the most suitable gap in the sentences below:

excuse	forgive	acquit	reprieve
absolve	overlook	exonerate	reconcile

I hope you will ______ and forget.
The Home Secretary ______ the murderer.
He was able to ______ the two friends who had quarrelled.
The teacher decided to ______ Smith's fault that time.
The jury ______ him of the offence.
The priest ______ him from his sins.
They ______ me of all blame in that unfortunate affair.
The pupil asked the teacher to ______ him from the lesson.

7) Rewrite the following passage inserting all Punctuation and Inverted Commas:

come along with me said the old woman and i will show you the bluebells are there really bluebells in this wood asked the little girl goodness me yes smiled the old lady they have been here for as long as anyone can remember and in the springtime at easter this wood is a sea of blue

THE ANIMALS CAME IN ONE BY ONE (I)

It was a pretty little place, set about with orchards and market gardens, with green open countryside down every wooded lane. There was a quiet little high street leading from the station to the green, and swans sailed like galleons on the pond.

I would buy a pennyworth of aniseed balls from Miss Markham's Sweet Shop, gape open-mouthed at Madam Alaska, a refugee from the Russian Revolution, who would stump down the high street in a Cossack hat, high buttoned tunic and boots, and avoid Jack the Butchers, because Jack, they said, bit off puppy dogs' tails.

He did too. I once saw him do it. It was a primitive form of docking for which he charged a fee, but as a little boy I thought he did it because he was a Bad Man. I hated dogs to be docked by any method, but I have to admit that Jack's method, though crude and revolting, must have been moderately efficient.

It was a great place for gypsies and a gypsy king and queen lived in a caravan on the outskirts. I knew that if I was naughty the gypsies would carry me off because my mother had told me so, but I was fascinated by them all the same and I loved their annual fair that would transform little Feltham into a place of great excitement, danger and glamour. There was, as a rule, very little excitement, danger or glamour in Feltham.

As good children of the chapel we were strictly warned against going near the Parish Church. If a service was in progress we must look the other way.

As it happened, the vicarage drew me irresistibly. The attraction, not felt by any of the vicar's parishioners or even by the unfortunate vicar himself, was the vicar's wife's herd of pedigree goats.

Mrs Bromwell, the vicar's wife, was a brusque, mannish lady who was never seen in church.

Her life revolved round these goats, much to the discomfort of her husband. They were, I thought, beautiful animals but they certainly made the vicarage smell. Even I noticed that. It was, without question, the smelliest vicarage in Middlesex.

Though I hated and feared the butcher's shop I loved the dairy, run by Mr. and Mrs. Mobbs who had their own cows and made their own butter. Mr. Mobbs taught me how to milk cows and Mrs. Mobbs how to operate the butter churn and they would deliver their fresh milk themselves, clip-clopping along the village streets and through the lanes to the bigger houses on a brightly painted milk cart.

Mr. Mobbs wore a celluloid eye patch and, for a treat, would raise it to show me the livid scar that it hid. His eye, he would say, had been shot out by the Germans. The Germans, I thought, had had a cheek to shoot at Mr. Mobbs.

It seems very odd to me now, but my father used to pay the local tradesmen only once a year. I can't imagine why they allowed him to owe them so much for so long, but he was a formidable man, not to be crossed lightly.

It was a useful arrangement for me. Mr. and Mrs. Mobbs sold delicious doughnuts and ice-creams and for some months I would take my playmates there and treat them. "My father says please put it on his account," I used to say. I remember my sinking heart the day the Mobbs' bill finally arrived. It was a long bill. Perhaps he wouldn't notice my small contribution. But of course he noticed. "What's this?" he snapped as he carefully checked the list. "And this?" And this?" The carpeting that followed left me a sadder and wiser child. It was, indeed, so shattering that I've never liked either cream or cream cakes ever since.

From "The Animals Came in One by One" by Buster Lloyd-Jones

COMPREHENSION

1) Name the five adjectives used in the first sentence of the passage.
2) Identify the simile used in the first paragraph.
3) Jack, they said, bit off puppy dogs' tails. Rewrite this in direct speech.
4) He was a "Bad Man". Why has the author given these words capital letters?
5) Explain, in your own words, the meaning of "crude and revolting" and "moderately efficient".
6) What is the name of the little town in the passage?
7) Give five idiomatic expressions from the passage.
8) Give one example of parenthesis from the passage.
9) What do you understand by "a carpeting"?

10) Explain, in your own words, the meaning of "sadder and wiser".
11) We know that the milk-cart was pulled by a horse. Give the word in the passage which tells us this.
12) How did the annual gypsy fair transform the little town?
13) Why did the author hate and fear the butcher's shop?
14) Did the vicar's parishioners like his wife's goats?
15) What, apart from milk, did Mr. & Mrs. Mobbs sell?
16) What was Mr. Mobbs' reason for wearing an eye-patch?
17) Why did the vicarage draw the author "irresistibly?"
18) What did the author buy from Miss. Markham?
19) What is the meaning of "charged a fee"?
20) What is a "market garden"?

RECAPITULATION

1) Rewrite the following passage inserting all missing Punctuation and Inverted Commas

it is remarkable how soon a baby senses ones meaning and responds some mothers instinctively realise this and we hear them talking to a tiny baby in this fashion come along baby its time for your bath or thats right kick away it makes your legs strong women who talk sensibly in this way as if the baby really understood always fare better in keeping the baby happy than those who treat the baby as a lifeless object to be bathed dressed and fed in silence

(From "Understanding Your Child" by Dr Winifred De Kok)

2) Write each of the Idiomatic expressions below in sentences of your own, to show that you understand their meaning:

An old head on young shoulders
His father's son
To cross someone
Sadder and wiser
To look the other way
Does not suffer fools gladly
To have a cheek
To be even-handed
Seen and not heard
To bring into the open

3) Combine each of the following pairs of sentences into one sentence by using conjunctions.

I pressed the button. The bell rang.
I am going to visit my friend. I have not seen her this week.
She did not blame him. She knew he was the culprit.
You should not eat your meal. You have washed your hands.
He was lost in the wood. The path had become overgrown.
I won't have any sweets, thank you. I like them very much.
Drink your coffee. It is still hot.
Will you make a decision? To come or not?

4) Rewrite the following sentences replacing the underlined words with Antonyms: (words of opposite meaning).

The wild creatures of the wood came confidently up to them.
The stag sprang merrily past them.
The birds ceased their songs.
They lay down on the mossy bank.
The car sped into a noisy street.
A polite servant opened the door.
The road to London is smooth and straight.
The princess was quiet and gentle.
She was famous for her generous and merciful rule.
He showed his brother gratitude and love.

5) Rewrite the following sentences filling the gaps with the appropriate Pronouns:

The teacher called out three children and told ______ to clear their desks.
In the game against you, ______ kept our heads but you lost ______.
Poor goslings! The wolf gobbled ______ all up!
When ______ had eaten his fill, ______ laid down and went to sleep.
The dog could not please himself; ______ had to guard the house and eat what his master gave ______.
My pen is not here, because I took ______ to school.
Sally cannot find ______ book, but ______ said ______ left______ on the

table.
I don't have my ruler, because Tom asked for ______ and I gave ______ to______.
Lucy wore her new hat in the rain and ______ is spoilt.
I cannot see Sophie, have you met ______?
We brought the bag in which ______ put the food.

6) Rewrite the following sentences choosing the correct word from the two Homophones inside the brackets:

She likes to (lay, lie) in bed.
Parcel up (their, they're) books.
We'll have brightly coloured flowers in the (border, boarder).
Go before (your, you're) discovered.
Your dress should be quite (all right, alright).
(There, They're) no longer in the cupboard.
He has (all ready, already) planted it.
It must be done, (weather, whether) it is (write, right) or wrong.
The farmer must (sheer, shear) his sheep.
Tell me (were, where) they are.
A (knave, nave) is part of a church.
Shall I (pear, pare) this apple for you?

7) Use one word to describe the following:

A rope for tying up a boat.
A place where money is kept.
The flesh of the pig.
To fight with gloves.
A man who makes clothes.
Twelve people trying a man in court.
A lady who sells flowers.
A family of puppies.
A ship that goes under water.
A wooden shoe.

THE LOST RACE

Scientists have long been puzzled about the great pyramids and giant statues, very old and beautiful, which can still be seen in Peru. The Incas, inhabitants of this part of South America, hundreds of years ago described the builders. They were, it seems, tall, white-skinned, blue-eyed and red-haired, a gentle, loveable people, and many of them skilled architects. Centuries ago they vanished from the American Continent. Where did they go?

The South Sea Islands, some three thousand miles off the Pacific Coast of South America, seem to contain the key to the mystery. In the first place ancient pyramids and statues very similar to those in Peru are to be found on some of the islands, and in addition those of the islanders who claim direct descent from the original settlers are white-skinned and blue-eyed. If these first settlers were, in fact, some of the lost race of Peru, how did they cross the vast ocean? In those far-off days they could hardly have had boats suitable for such a long voyage. Perhaps, thought some scientists, the American mainland was once joined to the islands and the long journey was made on foot. Zoologists, however, disproved this theory by showing that the animals to be found in both places were widely different. If the mysterious lost race had really reached the South Sea Islands they must have sailed there. In his famous book, the Kon-Tiki expedition, a young Norwegian scientist called Thor Heyerdahl tells how, with five courageous companions, he went to Peru and, using a light buoyant Peruvian wood called Balsa, built a large raft which they named "Kon-Tiki". Launching it on the Great Pacific Ocean, they drifted for three adventurous and perilous months before landing safely on one of the South Sea Islands. Such a voyage could have been made at any time in history. Has Heyerdahl solved the mystery of the lost race of Peru?

From "The Lost Race" By J. H. Duffy and H. Martin
(reprinted by permission of Robert Gibson and Sons, Glasgow, Limited)

COMPREHENSION

1) Describe the members of the Lost Race in your own words.
2) Give one example of parenthesis from the first paragraph and one example of parenthesis from the last paragraph.
3) How far from South America are the South Sea Islands?
4) What do Peru, and some of the South Sea Islands have in common?
5) Give one example of idiomatic speech from the second paragraph.
6) In the last paragraph there is one sentence which contains seven adjectives. Write down each of these adjectives.
7) Why did Thor Heyerdahl make the voyage to the South Sea Islands?
8) Which two adjectives show that the Kon-Tiki voyage was not an easy one?
9) Describe the great pyramids and giant statues which exist in Peru. Use words from the text.
10) Give four Proper Nouns from the first paragraph.
11) Give ten Common Nouns from the second paragraph.
12) Give five Proper Nouns from the last paragraph.
13) Describe the "Kon-Tiki" in your own words.
14) What kind of work is done by a zoologist? You may use your dictionary.
15) Give the reason why it is thought that the lost race must have sailed from Peru to the South Sea Islands. Use your own words.
16) How long would it have taken them to get there? Give your reason.
17) What kind of work is done by an Architect? You may use your dictionary.
18) Give the meaning of "claim direct descent" in your own words.
19) Rewrite "have long been puzzled" in your own words.
20) Explain, in your own words, the meaning of "the key to the mystery".

RECAPITULATION

1) Write down the <u>Prepositions</u> found in the following sentences and say which words each one relates:

He fell through the ice.
A stitch in time saves nine.
Lucy went with her father.
Jack jumped from here to there.
Behind me shone the sun.
He is different from his brother.
He took off his coat.
Divide the sweets between Jack and Lucy.
Liza apologised for her behaviour.
The master has authority over us.

2) Underline the Verbs in the following sentences:

They seem well and happy.
The end of the road came in sight.
Gardens beautify a school.
Liza is nearly always in the right.
Please tighten this screw for me.
Such a story will terrorise young children.
Shoot straight for the target.
His turn came to relieve the guard.
We need to enlarge the building.
The enemy will encircle the town.

3) Rewrite the following passage and underline each Adjective:

I think they were sad and lonely: an east wind blew from the stormy grey sea, there was a slight sprinkling of snow on the moor, the bracken was dead and brown, the heather was withered, only the prickly furze was still green with a yellow blossom here and there.

4) Write out the following sentences and underline each Pronoun:

Not only were we cold, but hungry.
Is the present for me?
A selfish child pleases only himself.

Yours is the bigger slice.
What a price you have paid!
Are the children by themselves?
That book is larger than mine.
Thou shalt not steal.
The judges voice sounded harsh to us.
I refuse to repeat the sentence.

5) Change the following passage from indirect to direct speech. Remember you will need to use Inverted Commas:

My landlady told me that I had chosen an excellent place for my convalescence. The weather, she assured me, was consistently mild. Indeed, although it was then mid-November, there had been no frost so far, either morning or evening. The local residents, too, were as kindly as the climate, and visitors were everywhere accepted and made welcome. She was sure that after a short stay among them I should have completely recovered from my recent serious illness. At that very moment, she added with a smile, she had a dinner ready for me that could not fail to bring back my lost appetite.

6) Using the following Conjunctions in the appropriate places, join each pair of sentences to make one sentence:

because than as soon as if that where until

My mother says. I must stay at home.
I know this is the man. I have seen him before.
I shall come to school tomorrow. My cold is better.
No one could find out. He had left his umbrella.
You must wait here. I come back.
He left the house. The rain stopped.
I would rather have a new pen. Take money to spend.

7) Rewrite the following sentences underlining each Adverb:

The house was conveniently situated just outside the town.
The child crept nervously down the dark stairs.

The hero strode valiantly to the fight.
The starved dog ate the food ravenously.
A wise man speaks modestly on all occasions.
The mother sang softly to her sleeping child.
She stepped quietly onto the stage and began to sing sweetly.
As the monster rushed at him, he nimbly stepped aside.

ELIZABETH I MEETS RALEIGH

Queen Elizabeth I was very fond of being outdoors. She had a very beautiful rose-garden in which she took great pleasure and in which she loved to walk at all times of day, but especially in the morning. This was when the roses smelled sweetest and still carried the early morning dew upon their petals.

Her favourite way of taking an airing, however, was by sailing on the River Thames. Almost every day, when the weather was favourable, seated in a splendid, velvet-cushioned barge, surrounded by her ladies-in-waiting, nobles and gentlemen of her court, she could be seen sailing in state gracefully along the river. Many of her subjects would watch this magnificent spectacle from the river-banks and marvel at the sight, hurrying later, to tell their neighbours of the queen's extravagant gown, her many jewels, the pearls worn in her hair; of Lord this, and Lady that, of who had accompanied her and who had not, and no detail would be missed out in the telling!

One morning the barge had approached the landing-place - the exquisitely-dressed queen had stepped out, and followed by her usual retinue of courtiers and ladies-in-waiting, dressed in their satin and velvet finery, proceeded towards the palace. A heavy rain had fallen during the night and left the ground muddy and sodden. At one spot which was particularly squelchy the queen hesitated for a moment.

A group of young gentlemen observed this and one of them, Walter Raleigh by name, hastily flung off the richly-embroidered, fur-trimmed cloak which he wore, and, stepping forward, gracefully spread it on the muddy ground before the queen. Elizabeth blushed, then, glancing for an instant at the noble figure of the young man to whom she was indebted for such a wonderful foot-cloth, passed over and proceeded on her way.

When Elizabeth reached the palace she at once despatched a messenger to look for the handsome young gentleman wearing a dirty cloak. Raleigh was summoned into the Royal presence and immediately taken into the service of Elizabeth. His handsome looks pleased the queen who loved to have such men about her court, while the sacrifice of his gorgeous mantle, made, as it was, with an air of devotion and gallantry, was well calculated to surprise and delight Elizabeth.

COMPREHENSION

1. Explain, in your own words, what is meant by "taking an airing".
2. Why did Raleigh spread his cloak on the ground?
3. When did Elizabeth most like to visit her rose-garden? Why was this?
4. Give the singular of "ladies-in-waiting".
5. What did Elizabeth's subjects hurry away to gossip about?
6. Which words tell us that the onlookers gossiped?
7. Why did Elizabeth blush?
8. Describe Raleigh's cloak.
9. When did Elizabeth send the messenger to find Raleigh?
10. Who did she tell him to look for?
11. How long was it before Raleigh was taken into the service of the queen?
12. What was it about Raleigh that pleased the queen?
13. Keeping the sense of the sentence, replace the words "was well calculated" with your own words.
14. Give three examples of parenthesis from the passage.
15. What does to "marvel at the sight" mean?
16. Explain the meaning of "magnificent spectacle."
17. How frequently did Elizabeth sail on the river?
18. Elizabeth "walked" in her rose garden. Find four more verbs in the passage which mean the same as (are synonymous with) "walk."
19. Give your own words for "usual retinue."
20. Give six adjectives from the passage.

RECAPITULATION

1. Re-write the following sentences <u>replacing the underlined phrases</u> with a single word of your own:

Elizabeth normally went for a walk <u>every day</u>.
She was accompanied by the <u>ladies, nobles and gentlemen</u> of her court.
Walter Raleigh, <u>without a moment's hesitation</u> took off his cloak.
He stepped <u>to the front</u> and spread it <u>with great care</u> on the ground.

There were eight people who were trying for the prize.
A good number of them were clothed in the livery of the queen.
Among the people who were watching was a young gentleman.
Elizabeth blushed as she put the question.
She wanted the gentleman to give an exhibition of his skill.
On no occasion did the young man make a complaint.

2. The following similes have become "mixed". Re-write them correctly:

as fit as horses
as old as a fiddle
as cool as a berry
as firm as a judge
as solemn as a cucumber
as like as the hills
as safe as a deer
as brown as two peas
as true as an owl
as swift as steel

3. Rewrite the following sentences inserting all Capital Letters, Punctuation and Inverted Commas:

1. oliver advanced slowly and said if you please sir i would like some more
2. the master was amazed but managed to shout what on earth do you mean
3. please sir replied oliver i want some more
4. mr bumble, mr bumble oh mr bumble sir come quick
5. mr bumble i beg your pardon sir but oliver twist has asked for more
6. what said mr limbkins at length in a faint voice
7. the beadle said what is your name boy
8. the master said i have never heard the likes of it
9. im glad it wasnt me who asked for more whispered one pauper to his friend
10. i know what you mean his friend replied i feel glad it wasnt me

4. Rewrite the following phrases, changing the words underlined so that the phrases have opposite meanings. (Replace with Antonyms).

The first week
A Summer apple-tree
A fine morning
A rough voice

A stout woman
The worse for you
A friendly farmer
A clever boy
A delicate girl
A generous uncle
An easy exercise
An unhappy story

A young thief
A perfect set of teeth
A serious accident
A valuable dog
A lively boy
A mean aunt
An exciting book
A sincere apology

5. Write out each of the following Idioms in a separate sentence of your own to show that you understand its meaning:

To draw the long bow.
A cock and bull story.
A storm in a teacup
The thin end of the wedge.
To show the white feather.

A last-ditch stand.
To sail close to the wind.
To tighten one's belt.
To send someone to Coventry.
The widow's mite.

6. Underline the Verbs in the following sentences:

Donkeys bray loudly but sometimes they give us rides on their backs.
The rain falls all day and I wish the sun shone.
The farmer trotted on his horse then they jumped the hedge into the meadow.
The sun is shining in the sky, the birds are singing in the trees.
He slipped on a patch of ice and fell flat on his face!
He planted wheat the first year and harvested all the grain.
I am doing a good thing growing crops on the hillside.
They picked the flowers and smelled their wonderful scent.
What do you mean by waking me up?
I do not have much to eat, but I am able to rest.

7. Rewrite the following, changing all the singular Nouns to Plural Nouns and vice versa:

coat babies witches brush
bricks lady bushes girls

boys	flies	fairies	puppy
birds	star	branches	porch
face	bridge	noses	pennies
duty	days	monkeys	wolves

THE ANIMALS CAME IN ONE BY ONE (II)

Neither my father nor my mother could ever believe that anyone was ever ill. They never seemed to be ill themselves and if my sisters or I said we didn't feel very well they immediately assumed we were malingering.

"Now then," my father would say briskly, "none of that....".

He was a great believer in physical exercise and plenty of fresh air and he saw to it that we got plenty of both. He was particularly keen on my taking full part in all wolf cub activities and was looking forward to seeing me march away to the annual wolf cub camp.

On the morning of the march I felt awful. I said so. My father was exasperated. "Now then," he said, "none of that," and hauled me smartly out of bed.

I felt worse and worse but my pack was strapped on my back and I was hurried off to join the other little boys. The camp was to be at a neighbouring village called Hatton, not very far away, in a field owned by a friend of my father's. It seemed like the end of the world to me that day.

We got there, at last, and then I found we were expected to swim in the river. I obediently undressed, got into my swimming costume, dragged myself to the river bank and jumped in. The water was running quite fast, rushing into a weir a little way downstream and almost at once I was in trouble.

I felt myself being tugged further and further towards the terrifying weir and suddenly I was in a whirlpool, swirling round and round and feeling cold hands dragging me under. I screamed. Then strong adult hands were pulling me to safety.

I was dried and put to bed and the cub master anxiously looked at me. "What are all those spots?" he said. No-one knew. "Better send for his father" said the cubmaster.

My father arrived, furious at all the fuss and I was taken home in the deepest disgrace and put to bed. My mother was impatient too, but she sent for a doctor who took one look at me and diagnosed scarlet fever. In the next two weeks the entire troop went down with scarlet fever too. I had generously passed it on to them all.

This was an ordinary enough illness of childhood and I was soon trying to be my father's son again. We could never take anything up like ordinary children. We had to be perfect, to outdo all the other children in the neighbourhood. So we had a coach for tennis, an instructor for riding and another for skating and another for swimming. Normally I would have enjoyed them all - but with my father in the foreground urging us on there was no fun in any of it. Games of any kind became a duty and a drudgery.

Just behind the tennis court was a sunken Italian garden. This had been built by enemy prisoners during the war and very splendid it was with its formal pools and fountains and flower beds.

Most of it was paved and this made it ideal for roller-skating. Furthermore, just by turning round in his umpire's chair, my father could supervise the Italian court too and so skating lessons became as great an ordeal as tennis. "Straighten your shoulders, Betty," my father would shout, "try to be a bit more graceful, John. KEEP YOUR BALANCE. Terrible!"

One day I was being taught a step that seemed to be terribly complicated. The instructor was shouting one set of instructions, my father was shouting another. I was skating along, trying to remember what to do with my feet, left over right, right over left, when suddenly I was down with a crash and there was a sharp pain in my leg.

"Get up, Get up," bellowed my father. "don't be such a silly boy. Get ON with it...."

I couldn't get on with it though. I'd broken my leg. My father was furious.

It was set by our elderly family doctor in a little back room under gaslight - set very badly as it turned out. In another six weeks another doctor looked at it and immediately had it re-set, which added six weeks to the time it took to recover. I never did learn that roller-skating step and there was to be very little skating or tennis or any other game for me in the years ahead.

From "The Animals Came in One by One" by Buster Lloyd-Jones.

COMPREHENSION

1. Give the meaning of the word "malingering". You may use your dictionary.
2. What is the simile the author uses to show how far away the field seemed to be? (paragraph 4).

3. Keeping the sense of the sentence, rephrase, in your own words "I was in trouble".
4. Give the metaphor the author uses to describe the sensation he felt in the whirlpool.
5. What is meant by "in the deepest disgrace"?
6. The author uses the idiom "trying to be my father's son". What does this expression mean?
7. Describe, in your own words, the author's father.
8. Where was the annual wolf cub camp?
9. Describe three features contained in the Italian garden.
10. Who built the Italian garden?
11. Give the name of one of the author's sisters.
12. What were the little boy's spots a symptom of?
13. How many different coaches did the author and his sisters have and what sports were these for?
14. What caused the author to fall and break his leg?
15. How long did it take altogether for the broken leg to heal?
16. Which is the single adjective the author uses to describe his mother?
17. Give, in your own words the author's opinion of games.
18. From the passage find eight adjectives.
19. Give three words the author uses to express how he felt about games.
20. Give one example of parenthesis from the passage.

RECAPITULATION

1. Give one word for the following:

A place sick people are taken to be healed.
A lady who makes and sells hats.
A man who sells fish.
A great number of bees.
A shop which sells newspapers.
A man who performs operations.
To make a noise like a lion.
The young of a kangaroo.

An implement for digging with.
A building made entirely of glass, used for raising plants.

2. Rewrite the following sentences and underline each Adverb:

The monster fled, bellowing wildly.
The cries of the wild birds echoed dolefully.
The man lay down and slept sweetly.
He narrowly escaped being killed.
He keenly felt the effects of the long chase.
The work in her book was neatly presented.
The journey went smoothly with no adventures.
She gently soothed her child to sleep.
Speak quietly or you will wake her.
She dances quite beautifully.

3. Write out the following sentences supplying the necessary Verbs to fill the gaps:

A hedgehog ________ in the wintertime.
A spider ________ a wonderful web.
In the Autumn, Swallows ________ to South Africa.
Have you ________ blackberries to ________ jam.
Very few insects are ________ in the winter.
Snowflakes ________ to the ground.
The bird was being ________ by the cat.
________ some seeds in the flower border.
When birds ________ they ________ their first song of the day.
Once baby birds ________ the nest they never go back.

4. Rewrite the following sentences inserting all the necessary punctuation:

please paint me blue said the cornflower
i like red best observed the poppy
why are your flowers still green asked a butterfly
the creeper replied oh dear i was too shy to stretch out my stalk

i am nearly scorched muttered the rock
this heat is terrible he groaned
she said to herself i will cover him with my leaves
how foolish i have been he cried
so were we all laughed the cornflower and the poppy
we will bow our heads they said and hide from the sun

5. An Adjectival phrase is a group of words doing the work of an Adjective, as:

A man in need - a needy man

Rewrite the following sentences replacing each underlined adjectival phrase with an adjective of similar meaning:

A thing of beauty is a joy for ever.
This is a matter of importance.
The material with the spots was very attractive.
The house on the corner belongs to my friend.
We are going for a holiday in the country.
The girl with the red hair won the contest.
The buckled knife was of no use.
His was a life without an aim.
I am a beggar without a penny.
We discovered a tunnel beneath the earth.

6. Not twenty yards from the window runs a honeysuckle hedge, and close to the top of a pair of linnets had, with great cunning, built their nest and hatched their little brood.

From the sentence above find:

One common noun.
One abstract noun.
Two adjectives and the nouns they qualify.
Two conjunctions and the parts of the sentence they join.
One example of parenthesis.

7. Form Nouns from the following list of Verbs. For example:

To consider	- Verb	=	consideration	- Noun (abstract)
To like	- Verb	=	liking	- Noun

to heighten	to decide	to pity	to endanger
to lengthen	to progress	to humour	to sympathise
to dry	to consider	to attend	to frighten
to cool	to forget	to change	to include

THE ANIMALS CAME IN ONE BY ONE (III)

When I was not busy coaxing wild animals in I lay for hours watching the wild life of the garden and, as the seasons slowly passed, I gradually began to make sense of what I saw and to understand how nature takes care of its own.

There were the pigeons in the elderberry trees when the fruit was ripe, their breasts stained with the purple juices. It wasn't just that they LIKED elderberries. They were, in fact, storing iron for the winter.

Then there were our cats. Why on earth were they eating that couch grass again? They must know it always made them sick. But of course - that was the whole point. They had a stomach ache and NEEDED to be sick.

And here came Paddy, leaping on to the bed and stinking of garlic. How could he gorge himself on that wild garlic that grew all over the garden and was cursed by the gardeners? Well he could because he had to. He had worms and the wild garlic was the certain cure. Now there he was rooting among the wild parsley, chewing it with the air of a small boy taking cod liver oil. He knew that the wild parsley would help to put his kidneys in order. Now I knew it too.

I could hardly realise it then, lying paralysed, but my real education had begun. Later I was to have a governess of my own and later still a succession of teachers. But my best and most valuable teachers were the birds in the trees, the wild life in the undergrowth and my own pets in the garden. I am still learning from them.

They have an instinctive wisdom, a deeply ingrained understanding of nature, which men once had, too. We have lost it and so, curiously enough, have many dearly loved domestic pets. You will never meet a fat tiger. But you do meet poodles, dachshunds, even alsations grown fat, flabby and ill through years of over-indulgence. Theirs is too valuable an inheritance to throw away and so, over the years, I have tried to salvage what I could. As a result I have been able to cure animals of all kinds of the diseases of civilisation. It was other animals who taught me how.

From "The Animals Came in One by One", by Buster Lloyd-Jones.

COMPREHENSION

1. Name one of the "diseases of civilisation".
2. Which word tells us that the author was unable to move.
3. Why did the pigeons eat the elderberries?
4. Give the reason why the cats ate the couch grass.
5. What is a certain cure for worms in dogs?
6. Which herb will help a dog's kidneys?
7. How did the animals and birds know what to eat?
8. Which phrase tells us that the author was bedridden for a very long time?
9. Describe what you think would be "the air of a small boy taking cod liver oil".
10. Give three of the author's "most valuable teachers".
11. Give another word (of your own) for "over-indulgence".
12. Explain, in your own words, the meaning of "too valuable an inheritance to throw away".
13. Explain, in your own words, "I have tried to salvage what I could".
14. Give, from the passage, one example of Parenthesis.
15. What does the author mean by "my real education had begun"?
16. From the passage give three abstract nouns.
17. From the passage give six common nouns.
18. From the passage give one proper noun.
19. From the passage give four adverbs.
20. From the passage give eight adjectives.

RECAPITULATION

1. Form Adjectives from the following list of verbs: for example:

To consider	-verb =	considerable	- Adjective
To like	-verb =	likeable	- Adjective

to heighten	to decide	to pity	to endanger
to lengthen	to progress	to humour	to sympathise
to dry	to consider	to attend	to frighten
to cool	to forget	to change	to include

2. Give one word for the following:

A tree or shrub which has green leaves all winter.
A sleeping- place for birds.
Mushrooms, toadstools and moulds.
A person who studies plants or animals.
A tree which bears cones.
A group of stars.
A sand hill.
Animals which eat flesh.
Animals which eat plants.
Warm-blooded animals with fur.

3. Write each of the Idiomatic expressions below in sentences of your own to show that you understand their meaning:

To save one's neck
To save for a rainy day.
By word of mouth.
To tip the wink.
A snake-in-the-grass.
To catch a glimpse of.
At first sight.
By all means.
On no account.
For your eyes only.

4. A mole burrows. A trout swims. Give the "movement" verbs to fill the gaps in the following:

A rabbit h________.
A river f________.
A horse g________.
A kangaroo h________.
A deer r________.
A toad w________.
A snake s________.
A fish s________.
A bird f________.
A frog l________.
A spider s________.
A cheetah r________.

5. Rewrite the following sentences changing the singular nouns and verbs into the plural;

One boy was in and the other was out.
Standing in the meadow was a pretty little house.
There was only one pale yellow primrose.
Lucy was a very pretty girl.
I do not know where he is.
The dog was at home all the time.
The dog is tired and the cat is hungry.
The book is green with red writing on its cover.
The girl has mumps so she is not at school today.
The horse was old and the master has left.

6. Rewrite the following sentences changing the plural nouns and verbs into the singular:

The boys are noisy, dirty and rough.
The desks were dirty and untidy.
The babies have chickenpox and are feeling poorly.
The hens were fat, sleek and happy.
The fairies have a magical time.
The two animals measured themselves.
When the guests had eaten, the sultan asked them to dance.
The guests knew the money would jingle in their pockets.
All your other guests have robbed you.
The guests came to three steps.

7. An Adverbial phrase is a group of words doing the work of an adverb as:

with great skill	-	skilfully
by fair means	-	fairly
in the garden	-	there
after a long time	-	eventually
in which street	-	where?

Rewrite the following sentences replacing each underlined Adverbial phrase with an Adverb of similar meaning:

I practised the piano with regularity.
The criminal obtained the money by dishonesty.
I will do it at this instant.
We live in this road.
They live in that road.
It has not rained during the last few days.
By slow degrees we removed the great boulder.
Do this at once!
She arranged the flowers in a haphazard fashion.
The assistant answered in a courteous manner.

ALL CREATURES GREAT AND SMALL (I)

I rang the doorbell and instantly the afternoon peace was shattered by a distant baying like a wolf pack in full cry. The upper half of the door was of glass and, as I peered through, a river of dogs poured round the corner of a long passage and dashed itself with frenzied yells against the door. If I hadn't been used to animals I would have turned and run for my life. As it was I stepped back warily and watched the dogs as they appeared, sometimes two at a time, at the top of their leap, eyes glaring, jaws slavering. After a minute or two of this I was able to sort them out and I realised that my first rough count of about fourteen was exaggerated. There were, in fact, five; a huge fawn greyhound who appeared most often as he hadn't so far to jump as the others, a cocker spaniel, a scottie, a whippet and a tiny, short-legged hunt terrier. This terrier was seldom seen since the glass was rather high for him, but when he did make it he managed to get an even more frantic note into his bark before he disappeared.

I was thinking of ringing the bell again when I saw a large woman in the passage. She rapped out a single word and the noise stopped as if by magic. When she opened the door the ravening pack was slinking round her feet ingratiatingly, showing the whites of their eyes and wagging their tucked-in tails. I had never seen such a servile crew.

"Good afternoon," I said with my best smile. "My name is Herriot."

The woman looked bigger than ever with the door open. She was about sixty but her hair, tightly pulled back from her forehead, was jet black and hardly streaked with grey. She nodded and looked at me with grim benevolence, but she seemed to be waiting for further information. Evidently, the name struck no answering spark.

From "All Creatures Great and Small", by James Herriot.

COMPREHENSION

1. What shattered the afternoon peace?
2. What could the author see as he peered through the glass of the front door?

3. Give one example of simile from the first paragraph and one from the second paragraph.
4. How many dogs did the author first think there were?
5. How many dogs were actually in the hall?
6. Name the breed of each of the dogs.
7. Give one example of Metaphor from the first paragraph.
8. She "rapped out" a single word. Explain this in your own words.
9. What does the author mean by "ravening" pack? You may use your dictionary.
10. Using your dictionary, find the meaning of the word "ingratiating". Then re-write, in your own words, the phrase "slinking round her feet ingratiatingly".
11. Explain, in your own words, the meaning of "grim benevolence".
12. In the last line, the author uses the word "evidently". Suggest another word he could have used in its place.
13. Why did the greyhound appear at the glass more often than the other dogs?
14. The name "struck no answering spark." Put this phrase into your own words.
15. Which word, in the first paragraph, tells us that the author felt a little nervous of the dogs?
16. Give the reason why the author did not turn and run for his life.
17. Explain the meaning of "a servile crew".
18. Describe the woman who answered the door, in your own words.
19. Keeping the sense of the sentence re-write "dashed itself with frenzied yells against the door". Use your own words.
20. Give ten verbs from the first paragraph.

RECAPITULATION

1. Re-write the following sentences inserting Capital Letters, Punctuation, and Inverted Commas wherever necessary:

dont bother about her said the breeder
shes in a bad way i said but she deserves a chance

oh just put her to sleep the breeder snapped
but we may be able to pull her through i said
dont waste time said the breeder put her to sleep and have done with it
at that i lost my temper
frankly i said id rather put you to sleep
how dare you talk to my wife like that he shouted
i told him how i dared i told him what i thought of him and his wife
oh shut up peter he would say oh shut up peter

2. The following Proverbs have become "mixed". Re-write them correctly:

Do not look , no bread.
A burnt child fears the kettle black.
One swallow does not make you leap.
Half a loaf is better than a gift horse in the mouth.
Look before you make a summer.
The pot calling the fire.
Out of debt and he'll take a yard.
A drowning man blames his tools.
Out of danger, give him an inch.
It's a bad workman who will clutch at a straw.

3. Re-write the following sentences replacing each underlined Adjectival phrase with an Adjective of similar meaning:

I met a beggar without a penny.
He was a man with a bad temper.
We came across a castle in ruins.
She seemed to be a woman of middle age.
The house next to us is being painted.
The hills in the distance were blurred.
It was the man with one leg again.
I want you to recommend a firm with a good reputation.
He is a pupil with intelligence.
She is a woman of learning.

4. Re-write the following sets of sentences as single sentences using a Conjunction from the list. Each Conjunction may only be used once, so it is important to choose the appropriate one for each set of sentences:

therefore	because	however	unless	since
also	nevertheless	although	before	whilst

My fingers are stiff and cramped. I find writing difficult.
I am cold and tired. I would like to go home now.
I cannot reach the shelf. It is too high.
He wants to come. He must remain here.
He has been very naughty. I will not punish him.
She won the race. She was not completely fit.
Tomorrow's outing will be fun. It is raining.
I wish you had told me the meeting was cancelled. I set off.
I will come with you. You asked me so politely.
I will make the tea. They clear up all the mess.

5. Give one word for the following:

Frozen rain, falling to the earth in small, hard lumps.
A man who studies rocks.
Animals which have a backbone.
Animals which do not have a backbone.
A place where ships are built.
Remains or imprints of once-living things found in rocks.
A number of whales.
A glass tank in which tropical fish are kept.
A four-footed animal.
A group of sheep.

6. Make Adverbs from the following list of verbs, for example:

To consider - verb = considerably - adverb

to heighten	to decide	to pity	to endanger

to lengthen	to progress	to humour	to sympathise
to dry	to consider	to attend	to frighten
to cool	to forget	to change	to include

7. Give the plural of the following Nouns:

bully	match	empress	baby
valley	ox	worry	mouse
donkey	jelly	torch	chimney
trout	dormouse	sheep	army
leaf	shelf	roof	cliff
calf	dwarf	passer-by	boy-scout

ALL CREATURES GREAT AND SMALL (II)

" We'll go home a different way." Farnon leaned over the driving wheel and wiped the cracked windscreen with his sleeve. "Over the Brenkstone Pass and down Sildale. It's not much further and I'd like you to see it."

We took a steep, winding road, climbing higher and still higher with the hillside falling away sheer to a dark ravine where a rocky stream rushed headlong to the gentler country below. On the top, we got out of the car. In the summer dusk, a wild panorama of tumbling fells and peaks rolled away and lost itself in the crimson and gold ribbons of the western sky. To the east, a black mountain overhung us, menacing in its naked bulk. Huge, square-cut boulders littered the lower slopes.

I whistled softly as I looked around. This was different from the friendly hill country I had seen on the approach to Darrowby.

Farnon turned towards me. "Yes, one of the wildest spots in England. A fearsome place in winter. I've known this pass to be blocked for weeks on end."

I pulled the clean air deeply into my lungs. Nothing stirred in the vastness, but a Curlew cried faintly and I could just hear the distant roar of the torrent a thousand feet below.

It was dark when we got into the car and started the long descent into Sildale. The valley was a shapeless blur but points of light showed where the lonely farms clung to the hillsides.

From "All Creatures Great and Small" by James Herriot

COMPREHENSION

1) With what did Farnon wipe the windscreen?
2) What route home did Farnon suggest they take?
3) They reached the top at sunset. We know this because the author has written a particularly good metaphor to tell us this. What is the metaphor?
4) Make up a metaphor of your own to descibe a sunset. Do not use

words from the passage.

5) The author speaks of "down Sildale" and "long descent into Sildale". What is Sildale?
6) What does the author mean by the "gentler" country below?
7) Why does the author describe the mountain as "menacing"?
8) What does the author mean by "naked bulk"? Rephrase this in your own words. Why does he use the word "naked"?
9) What made the author whistle softly as he looked around?
10) What kind of countryside had the author seen on the approach to Darrowby?
11) How did Farnon describe the Brenkstone Pass?
12) Which bird could they hear crying faintly?
13) How high up were they when they got out of the car?
14) Which adjective tells us that there were not many farms?
15) From the last paragraph, give two adjectives.
16) From the fourth paragraph, give two adjectives.
17) What could the author hear from the top of the Brenkstone Pass?
18) Change the first paragraph from direct to indirect (reported) speech.
19) Using your dictionary, give the meaning of the word "panorama".
20) Explain in your own words what "a dark ravine" is.

RECAPITULATION

1) Rewrite the following sets of sentences using a Conjunction from the list below. Each Conjunction may only be used once, so it is important to choose the appropriate one for each set of sentences:

either	after	until	in case
neither	when	whether	where
while	even so		

I cannot decide. To come with you or not.
I do not like Amy. Do I like Lucy.
You can choose. To play tennis or to play rounders.
I will wait patiently. You make up your mind.
The pupils ran out of school. The bell rang.

I know you are sorry now. You still deserve to be punished.
We should take down the tent. It will rain tomorrow.
Shall we play a game of Monopoly. We have had our tea?
The little girl did not wait. Her mother had told her to stay.
I will play with you. It is time for me to go home.

2) Give the plural of the following Nouns:

girl	puppy	bush	pansy
fish	boat	wife	sheaf
wharf	thief	gulf	half
deer	wolf	echo	tomato
potato	negro	piano	solo
stepson	father-in-law	man-o'-war	cloth

3) Write each of the Idiomatic expressions below in sentences of your own, to show that you understand their meaning:

In a nutshell	All things considered
To keep it dark	To hold one's tongue
To blurt it out	Facing the music
To give the cue	To refuse to hear
To bear in mind	Before one's eyes

4) Read carefully the following sentences, then underline every Preposition:

I am not surprised that Lucy admired your dress because it is similar to hers.
It is different from mine since yours is blue with long sleeves.
My dress differs from yours since it is red with short sleeves.
Lucy made her own dress, being accomplished in dressmaking.
Compared with Hannah, Lucy is a beginner.
When Columbus sailed for America his crew decided to rebel against him.
The voyage was dependent on the generosity of the Queen of Spain.
I shall do this independent of any help from you.
At any rate I shall have only myself to blame if it should go wrong.
With the storm fast approaching they rowed for dear life.

5) Give one word for the following:

A group of people singing together.
A road with trees on both sides.
A person who walks instead of using transport.
The flesh of a sheep.
A list of dishes on a restaurant table.
A number of soldiers.
An animal which walks on two legs.
A place where coal is dug.
A very large group of trees.
A roof made of straw.

6) Rewrite the following sentences replacing each underlined Adverbial Phrase with an Adverb of similar meaning:

He faced the difficulty with courage.
The car nosed its way by slow degrees through the crowd.
The messenger entered in haste.
The ship sailed steadily towards the west.
You must do this question without hesitation.
Toby was found after a long search.
The children stayed in the garden.
He constructed the model with great skill.
In which street do you live?
She won the competition by fair means.

7) Give the Collective Noun for each of the following:

A collection of people in church
A great many stars
Many loaves, baked at the same time
A number of partridges
A collection of people in a theatre
A number of lions
A collection of books
A great many bullocks
The teachers in a school
The sailors on a ship

ANTONIO

A long way to the south of Great Britain lies the country of Italy. It is a lovely country, and has many beautiful cities. One of these cities is Venice. It is a city of the sea, because it is built on many islands joined together by bridges. The streets are canals and the people travel in boats, known as gondolas.

The men who built Venice were very rich, and they loved to have beautiful things around them. They built great churches and grand houses and filled them with lovely carvings and pictures.

Antonio was a little boy who lived near Venice nearly two hundred and fifty years ago. His father was a poor man who worked on a farm. One day Antonio found a lump of clay. He ran home with it. "Look mother," he cried "look what I have found! What fine castles and birds and flowers I shall be able to make now!" Antonio sat on the floor and began to mould the clay into all sorts of shapes. What a joy it was to him!

While he was working, a friend of his father came in. He was the cook at a grand house not far away. He seemed to be in trouble. "What is the matter?" asked Antonio's mother. "You know," said the cook, "that I am very clever at making beautiful shapes for the table. I can make castles, dragons, birds, trees and pretty flowers out of sugar and pastry. Tonight we are going to have a grand dinner. The master says I must make something for the table that he has never seen before. I cannot think of anything new. What shall I do?"

While the mother and the cook were talking, Antonio was busy making a little swan out of clay. When it was finished he put it on a corner of the table. The cook left the house. As he did so, he knocked down Antonio's little swan. "Oh my poor swan!" cried Antonio. "That clumsy man has ruined it. I shall never forgive him."

"You must not say that," said the mother. "He is in trouble today and he hardly knows what he is doing. His master has told him to make some new shapes for dinner tonight, and he cannot think of anything that he has not made already." "Oh!" said Antonio, "is that all? I will help him." The mother smiled, but the boy picked up his cap and set off for the great house.

He went to the kitchen and asked to see the cook. "If you don't mind," he said, "I have come to help you. Give me a big block of butter, and I will soon make you something new." "All-right," said the cook, "I know you will only spoil the butter, but you can try. Go into that little room, and call me when you have finished."

Antonio worked hard for three or four hours. Then he opened the door and called the cook. On the table stood a lion made out of butter! The lion looked almost as if it were alive. The cook could not believe his eyes. He stared at the lion and he stared at the boy. Then he shook Antonio by the hand. "You have saved me," he said.

The lion was placed in the middle of the table at dinner that night. When the master and his friends saw it they were amazed! "Send for the cook," they cried. "he is a great man!"

The cook came into the room, and the master praised him for his work. "No," said the cook, "do not praise me. I did not make the lion." "Then send for the man who DID make it," said the master.

Little Antonio was led into the room. You can imagine how surprised the master and his friends were. They could hardly believe that a poor little boy had made the magnificent lion.

The master was so pleased that he sent Antonio to school, and afterwards had him taught to carve in marble. When he grew up he carved many beautiful figures out of marble. Some of them may still be seen in the beautiful old city of Venice.

The full name of Antonio was Antonio Canova. He was born in 1757 and died in 1822. He carved such beautiful statues that in 1816 he was made a nobleman.

COMPREHENSION

1) In what way is Venice different from other cities?
2) What was Antonio doing when the cook came to his father's house?
3) What sort of things could the cook make out of sugar and pastry?
4) Why was the cook unhappy?
5) What sort of things did Antonio say he would be able to make with the clay?
6) How did Antonio help the cook?
7) Give the name of the boats people use to travel by, in Venice.
8) Why did Antonio say that he would never forgive the cook?
9) How long did Antonio spend working on the lion?

10) How did the master reward Antonio?
11) What final reward did Antonio's carving skills earn him?
12) What was Antonio's father's occupation? Was he rich?
13) What kind of men built Venice?
14) Where did Antonio place his finished swan?
15) What did Antonio ask the cook to give him?
16) One adjective is used five times in the passage. What is the adjective?
17) What was the cook's reaction when he saw the lion?
18) What did the cook say when the master praised him for his work?
19) Give five verbs from paragraph four.
20) Give four Proper Nouns from the first paragraph.

RECAPITULATION

1) Look carefully at the underlined words in the following sentences. Write out each of these underlined words and state whether they are an Adjective or an Adverb.

We watched the hilarious antics of the baby monkeys.
Altogether, it was a magical day out.
He glared at his enemy hatefully and malevolently.
He was ravenously gobbling up a huge plate of food.
She arrived wearing astoundingly magnificent jewels.
She was bored and showed it by yawning continuously.
We knew she was cross by her impatient gestures and angry face.
I like you because you are such a reliable friend.
My fingers are cramped and twisted with rheumatism.
Dance, Dance, gladly, merrily, joyfully!

2) Change the following sentences from direct to indirect (reported) speech. You will not use inverted commas, but remember you will need to change the pronouns and the tense.

Antonio cried, "That clumsy man has ruined it. I shall never forgive him."
"You must not say that." said the mother.
"Oh!" said Antonio, "is that all? I will help him."

"If you don't mind," he said, "I have come to help you."
The cook said "I know you will only spoil the butter, but you can try."
"You have saved me," he said.
"Send for the cook," they cried "he is a great man."
"No," said the cook, "do not praise me. I did not make the lion."
"Then send for the man who did make it ," said the master.
"Go into that little room, and call me when you have finished," said the cook.

3) Complete the following sentences inserting the correct Pronoun in each gap. Choose the <u>Pronoun</u> from the list below, you may use each one only once:

everybody	whom	these	which	others
myself	where	that	what	each

I made it ________ with no help from the teacher.
________ has a talent for something.
I am a hopeless skater. I leave ________ to the people who are clever on skates!
________ would you prefer, to walk or to cycle?
I cannot say my work is good, that is for ________ to decide.
Shakespeare was a playwright of ________ you must have heard.
________ in the world did you buy such an awful hat?
I don't usually enjoy strawberries, but ________ are especially juicy.
I know he lives in this road, but I'm not sure ________ is his house.
"To ________ his own", is a French proverb.

4. Rewrite the following sentences, underlining each <u>Noun</u> and say what kind of <u>Noun</u> each one is:

Because it was warm and sunny the children played outdoors.
She was in a thoughtful mood, remembering his kindness to her.
London is a busy, crowded fascinating city.
Our loft has been invaded by a swarm of bees.
When visiting the zoo we saw an elephant with her calf.
We also saw several hippopotami wallowing in the mud.

Comedians often make cruel jokes about mothers-in-law.
Harry and William are royal princes.
She exhibited great strength in overcoming her handicaps.
He fixed his enemy with a look of hatred.

5. Give <u>one word</u> for each pair of phrases, for example: A place where money is kept (A BANK) the edge of a river.

A very young cow.	Part of the leg.
A big stone.	Sway to and fro.
To fight with gloves.	A container.
To run away.	A lock on a door.
A herb.	A building where money is made.
Belonging to me.	A place where coal is dug.
The beak of a bird.	A tradesman's account.
A door fastening.	A piece of hair.
The opposite of heavy.	The opposite of dark.
The opposite of short.	To want very much.

6. Decide which of the following sentences contain <u>Similes</u> and which contain <u>Metaphors</u>:

I'm not fibbing, it's as true as I stand here!
She was like a cat on hot bricks.
He was a giant among men.
His word is his bond.
If you lie, you will be treading a dangerous path.
The train took forever to arrive.
He has the wisdom of Solomon.
The burglar was as silent as a cat.
He was so happy, he was like a dog with two tails.
She smelt as sweet as a rose.

7, Re-write the following sentences giving a synonym of your own to replace the underlined words:

A barge is a <u>vessel</u> which carries goods on a canal.

The sabres were given sharp points.
The willing helpers launched the boat.
They took the first train in the morning.
Fifteen children were rescued from drowning.
He took several shots at the deer.
In her mirror she saw strange visions.
They kept a special place for her.
The gift added to her pleasure.
A brilliant sun shone in the sky.

Remember true synonyms must be the same part of speech, that is, if you are using a synonym for a verb, your synonym must be another verb, a synonym for a noun must be another noun, a synonym for an adjective must be another adjective and so on.

JAYTEE PET HEROES (I)

Pam Smart of Ramsbottom, Lancashire, claims that her seven-year-old terrier mongrel dog, Jaytee, possesses a mysterious power. Her parents first noticed something unusual when they looked after Jaytee while Pam was at work. Long before she came home from work the dog went to wait by the window, but Pam put this down to a regular schedule which Jaytee had learnt. However, when Pam gave up her job as a school secretary in 1993 and started returning at irregular times, Jaytee would still walk over to the window when she was about to set off from her distant location. Pam's mother made a record of when the dog reacted and then compared the times to when Pam had left to return home, and, give or take a few minutes, they generally matched. Jaytee seemed to know the moment Pam prepared to leave for home.

Pam tried to look at it from a sceptic's point of view. "I thought it might be the sound of the car, so I went in Taxis or other people's cars. I even cycled and went on foot to rule that one out," she explained. She also ruled out any powerful sense of hearing because several times Jaytee has known when she was leaving Blackpool forty-five miles away and it's simply impossible that any dog could hear that far!

It was possible, however, that the dog might be picking up subtle cues from her parents, so Pam didn't tell them when she was returning home. But the results over three weeks of testing were still the same. Some people might say that the dog is telepathic and picks up Pam's thoughts, but she denies this: "It's nothing I feel - when I get in the car to come home I am not particularly thinking about Jaytee."

Biologist Dr Rupert Sheldrake in London has long had an interest in the powers of prediction of animals. He has now carried out 156 tests on Jaytee and found that he successfully anticipated Pam's return home 81 per cent of the time, no matter how long Pam had been away, or how long she had to travel home. The 19 per cent of the time the dog got it wrong were when he was distracted by visitors such as the postman, or friends.

To see whether noise could distract Jaytee, twenty-three experiments were made involving loud banging outside the house as a car was worked on in the street. Although Jaytee went to the window to investigate the commotion outside - which counted as a failure in these experiments - he still successfully predicted Pam's return home 68 per cent of the time.

During these tests, Dr Sheldrake also made sure that Pam couldn't inadvertently let Jaytee know her plans in advance by sending Pam randomly selected times to return home at a few moments' notice using a radio bleeper.

He also complemented these tests by using video cameras to record four-hour periods of Jaytee's behaviour to see when he gazed out of the window and whether this matched the time Pam set off. In two hundred hours of video recording, Jaytee showed a consistently high success rate. Even when Dr Richard Wiseman - a highly sceptic psychologist from Hertfordshire University - repeated the same tests himself, Jaytee scored two out of three successful predictions. This was essentially the same pass rate as Sheldrake's results. Wiseman, however, considered this proof of the dog's failure, which seems unduly harsh.

Another of Dr Sheldrake's test owners is Jan Fennel who believes her seven dogs know when she is thinking about taking them for a walk which they anticipate by becoming noisy, boisterous and making for the door. Even though the dogs have no set time for their outings and even though she can be in another part of the house where they can't see her, they still grow excited when she starts thinking about walking them. To test whether they really can read her mind, Jan locked her dogs in the conservatory for a few hours each day with a video camera recording their every movement, while she was in another part of the house doing things ranging from housework to watching television. Then, completely at random, she would spend ten minutes thinking of walking the dogs. Early results from the video seem to show that, at the moment Jan has these thoughts, the dogs jump towards the door and make a noise, having spent most of their time beforehand being fairly inactive. A lot more tests are needed before these results prove significant but early indications are intriguing.

Pam Smart's and Jan Fennel's experiences with their dogs are far from unique. Dr Sheldrake has collected about two thousand similar cases of pets predicting their owners' return, from Britain, France, Austria and the U.S.A., and they tend to have an uncannily similar pattern.

From "Pet Heroes" by Paul Simons

COMPREHENSION (1)

1. What is Jaytee's mysterious power?
2. Who first noticed the unusual happenings?
3. How did Pam prove that it was not the sound of her car which alerted Jaytee?
4. How do we know that it was not "any powerful sense of hearing" which alerted Jaytee?
5. What is Dr Rupert Sheldrake's occupation? Where does he work?
6. What is Dr Sheldrake's particular interest?
7. Name two of Dr Sheldrake's test owners.
8. How many tests has Dr Sheldrake carried out on Jaytee?
9. How often did Jaytee successfully anticipate Pam's return home?
10. What was the reason for Jaytee getting it wrong some of the times?
11. How old is Jaytee?
12. What breed of dog is Jaytee?
13. How many experiments were made to see whether noise could distract Jaytee?
14. What kind of noise was used to distract Jaytee and how was this noise produced?
15. How often did the dog successfully anticipate Pam's return in these "noise" tests?
16. How did Dr Sheldrake ensure that Pam couldn't let Jaytee know her plans?
17. Which two pieces of equipment were used in this experiment?
18. What is Dr Richard Wiseman's occupation? Where does he work?
19. How did Jaytee score in Dr Wiseman's tests?
20. What did Dr Wiseman consider these results to be proof of?

COMPREHENSION (II) (much harder!)

1. How many dogs does Jan Fennel own?
2. What power do Jan Fennel's dogs possess?
3. How did Jan set about testing this power?
4. Give three reactions which Jan's dogs have to her thoughts.

5. Why are Jan's test results not yet "significant"?
6. Give another word for "significant". You may use your dictionary.
7. How many similar experiences has Dr Sheldrake collected?
8. In which countries did Dr Sheldrake collect these experiences?
9. What is the meaning of "successfully anticipated"? (paragraph 4)
10. Using your own words, replace the idiom "completely at random".
11. Explain, in your own words, the meaning of "early indications are intriguing".
12. Using your dictionary, give the meaning of "complemented" and explain how it differs from the word "complimented". (paragraph 7)
13. Keeping the meaning of the sentence, replace the words "subtle cues" with words of your own. (paragraph 3)
14. What is the meaning of "randomly selected" in paragraph 6.
15. Using your dictionary, find the meaning of the word "uncanny" then put into your own words the phrase "uncannily similar pattern". (last line)
16. Use a dictionary to find the meanings of the following words: sceptic, telepathic, inadvertently. Write down the meanings.
17. What is the meaning of "consistently high" in paragraph 7?
18. From paragraph 7 of the passage, give one example of parenthesis.
19. When did Pam leave her job as a school secretary?
20. From paragraph 3 of the passage, find 4 conjunctions.

RECAPITULATION

1. Re-write the following passage, turning it from direct to indirect (reported) speech. Remember you will need to change the personal pronouns and the tense. You do not use inverted commas:

"I thought it might be the sound of the car, so I went in taxis or other people's cars. I even cycled and went on foot to rule that one out," she explained. "It's nothing I feel - when I get in the car to come home I am not particularly thinking about Jaytee." "He does not respond at all to my leaving one place and moving to another," she claims. "His response seems to be apparent at the time I think of returning home and walk towards my car to come home."

2. Give <u>one word</u> for each pair of phrases, for example:
A place where money is kept (a bank) the edge of a river.

A big animal with a shaggy coat.	To carry.
The back part of a ship.	Severe.
Shade for a window.	Unable to see.
Something you do in cricket.	A dish.
To dip the head suddenly.	A bird that swims.
A place where a corpse is put.	Very serious.
A tool used for gardening.	To gather.
To pick.	Courage.
Good to others.	Sort.
A kind of cricketer.	A kind of hat.

3. Re-write the following paragraph, changing from <u>indirect</u> to <u>direct</u> speech. You must use inverted commas where necessary and change the past tense to the present tense:

Some young elephants leapt playfully through the jungle. One of them slipped and slid on his back down a small incline for thirty yards, and knocked down a few trees on the way. He came to a halt, still on his back, and wagged his big head with laughter. He saw something small which moved on the ground. He asked what it was, in a mirthful voice. The little thing said in squeaky tones that it was a mouse. The elephant said wasn't it small? The mouse replied that it had been very ill.

4. Complete the following <u>proverbs</u>:

Better late ______ ______.
A miss is as good ______ ______ ______.
_____ _____ _____ is better than no bread.
______ ______ like son.
______ is better than cure.
______ ______ twice shy.
______ ______ has a silver lining.

_____ _____ _____ _____ flock together.
_____ _____ _____ _____ saves nine
_____ _____ half done.

5. Turn each of the following adjectives into verbs. For example:

Considerate	- adjective	=	Consider	- verb

ruined	beautiful	useful	patterned
lame	needy	dark	hardy
broad	wild	human	valid
bossy	shady	chilly	short
delightful	desirable	dreadful	light

6. Write out the following sentences underlining the Auxiliary verbs:

I will check what is on television tonight.
My brothers say I can dance really well.
I must clean the patio before the summer comes.
We were laughing so much, nobody knew why.
We have finished our homework.
Will running make my muscles ache?
Sarah has scored a high mark in her exam.
You should see the new film showing at the cinema.
Has exercise helped you to lose weight?
I should groom my cat regularly so that her fur does not become matted.

7. Re-write the following sentences inserting the correct Prepositions in the gaps:

The path _____ the wood makes a short cut _____ the village.
The canoe sank _____ the lake _____ the valley below.
They were _____ to their eyes _____ work.
I shall attend _____ your request _____ the earliest opportunity.
The cat _____ the tree was _____ difficulty.
_____ the glen rode armed men.
_____ doubt one might fall _____ thieves _____ one's journey _____ Europe _____ the dark ages.

Such behaviour is _____ contempt.
This is little different _____ the rest _____ the sentences.
_____ the rugged rock the ragged rascal ran.

ZIGGY AND STELLA PET HEROES (II)

Australian Women's Weekly reported a story of such superb co-ordination between a pair of dogs that it shows either that dogs have far better powers of communication than we suspect or that some dogs are telepathic.

In 1994, border collie Ziggy and rottweiler Stella teamed up to save their master Chris Georgiou from drowning. Chris was out on his farm on a cold September afternoon in the Adelaide Hills in Australia. By 5pm he was tired, having spent three hours cutting wild lilies from the banks of his trout lake. Clutching an iron rail in order to pull himself clear of the muddy bank, he accidentally banged his head against it, stunning himself. He lost his grip and slid into the icy water and because he could not swim he felt a rush of terror. He clawed madly at the slippery bank but he was heavily weighed down with overalls, a thick jumper, coat and gumboots and couldn't get a grip. "The dam was four metres deep and I was just thinking, I'm gone," Chris said. "My wife was overseas. There was nobody else around."

But faithful Ziggy was on the bank. "I could see him running back and forth. He was making a hell of a noise," said Chris. "It wasn't a bark but an unusual sort of cry. I'd never heard anything like it before." A moment later, getting close to his last breath, Chris felt a touch on his shoulder. It was Stella, his other dog who had waded in. "I hadn't seen her since lunchtime when I'd left her at the house. She's a lazy dog and she'd been asleep in her kennel!"

She had dived straight into the water and swum to reach Chris. Stella was a large dog, weighing about fifty-six kilograms, and Chris managed to get an arm around her body and haul himself a few metres away to where he knew there was a big log just below the water's surface. "I still don't know if I steered the dog towards it or the dog took me there. But I was able to stand up on it. From there, I could reach over to the dam wall. I pulled myself out by grabbing on to some wooden steps."

Somehow Ziggy must have communicated to Stella with his strange, high-pitched howl and Stella wasted no time arriving at the scene. "Ziggy is a very light dog. So I think he knew he couldn't do anything for me himself. But then, I had never seen Stella in the water before. Rottweilers are not water dogs. It makes what she did that much more heroic." Both dogs showed great qualities. Ziggy's instincts as a collie would normally be to protect his flock from trouble, but being too small to help he used his intelligence to seek help elsewhere and Stella's quick appreciation of the danger and decisive action shows the cleverness and bravery of Rottweilers.

From "Pet Heroes" by Paul Simons

COMPREHENSION

1) What was the name of the dog's master?
2) Whereabouts was his farm?
3) What breed of dogs were Ziggy and Stella?
4) At what time did the accident take place?
5) P.M. stands for "post meridiem". What does "post meridiem" mean in English? What language is it?
6) How did the accident happen?
7) What had Chris been doing before the accident?
8) How long had he spent at his task?
9) Why was Chris terrified that he might drown?
10) What was it that weighed him down?
11) Give another word for "gumboots", "overseas" and "bravery".
12) How did Ziggy communicate with Stella?
13) In your own words explain the meaning of "getting close to his last breath".
14) Replace the phrase "used his intelligence" with a phrase of your own.
15) What does the author mean by "Stella's quick appreciation of the danger"?
16) What is meant by "a rush of terror"?
17) How did Stella manage to save Chris?
18) Explain, in your own words, the meaning of "decisive action."
19) "Both dogs showed great qualities." What were the qualities the dogs showed?
20) How deep was the dam?

RECAPITULATION

1) Rewrite the following passage, turning it from direct to indirect (reported) speech Remember you will need to change the personal pronouns and the tense. Do not use inverted commas:

"The dam was four metres deep and I was just thinking, I'm gone," Chris said. "My wife was overseas. There was nobody else around." "I could see him running back and forth. He was making a hell of a noise," said Chris. "It wasn't a bark but an unusual sort of cry. I'd never heard anything like it before."

"I hadn't seen her since lunchtime when I'd left her at the house. She's a lazy dog and she'd been asleep in her kennel!" Chris remembered. "I still don't know if I steered the dog towards it or the dog took me there. But I was able to stand up on it. From there, I could reach over to the dam wall. I pulled myself out by grabbing on to some wooden steps."

2) Rewrite the following sentences underlining all the Conjunctions:

I hate cricket, although I love tennis.
I could not go out as I had a bad cold.
He hoped very much to be there in time, but it was in vain.
I raised my gun and the bird disappeared.
You can catch either a train or a bus.
She is very plump because she eats so many chocolates.
They gave two weeks' notice that they would be leaving.
Leave the light on because I am frightened of the dark.
I will leave the light on if you are afraid.
I was working well until I stopped for coffee!

3) Write out the following sentences underlining the Auxiliary Verbs:

The sun is setting in the west.
All the people would read my book.
A dozen crows were huddled together.
The fire was dying slowly.
I'm hurrying from the distant hills.

The lazy boy had been sleeping.
The referee blew the whistle.
The girl is writing a letter.
Tom has eaten his dinner.
I shall be telling the story again.

4) Give one word for each of the following:

My brother's daughter.
An unmarried man.
My sister's son.
My sister's husband.
All of the same opinion.
A number of whales.
A place where ships unload.
A man who sells fresh meat.
A lady who makes clothes for others.
Twenty-four sheets of paper.

5) Rewrite the following sentences underlining each Adverb:

I can only speak this well.
My mother always instructed me to tell the truth.
I am unable to say certainly when I am leaving.
I only saw him yesterday.
You may well say you did it.
Foolishly, I answered both questions.
The cat climbed down.
We saw a skylark hovering above.
"Come inside," shouted our friend.
A shabby figure sidled alongside, and began to whisper.

6) Write the following Idiomatic Expressions in sentences of your own to show that you understand their meaning:

unable to put two words together
facing the music
to cudgel one's brains
at the end of the day
by hook or by crook
having too many irons in the fire
on the sly
to be intent upon
when all is said and done
to keep a sharp look-out

7) Which <u>Homophones</u> should be used to fill the blank spaces in the following sentences?

The vote was _______ since everyone was of the same opinion. (unanimous, anonymous)
He is a truly _______ man. A real gentleman. (descent, decent)
How will this _______ my life? (effect, affect)
What _______ will this have upon my life? (affect, effect)
The poor old man walked with an uncertain _______ . (gate, gait)
The gypsy-girl _______ clothes-pegs and lace and lucky heather from a huge basket. (pedalled, peddled)
The pirate's _______ of gold coins was locked inside a treasure chest. (horde, hoard)
Our car was _______ when someone drove into the back of it. (stationery, stationary)
His _______ on the ocean liner was very comfortable. (birth, berth)
The cat fell from a sixth _______ balcony. (story, storey).

GREYFRIARS BOBBY PET HEROES (III)

Greyfriars Bobby's is probably the most famous story of dog loyalty. Bobby was a black skye terrier working with his shepherd Auld Jock, who herded sheep on Cauldbrae Farm in the Pentland Hills in southern Scotland. Every Wednesday they both went to market day in Edinburgh and at exactly 1 p.m. would go for lunch at Traill's Dining Rooms in Greyfriars Place nearby. Despite it being busy on a market day, the owner, John Traill, always spoke to Auld Jock with Bobby at his heels.

Then one day in 1858 Jock was sacked from his job. Jock was driven back to Edinburgh Grassmarket to get him well away from the farm where he was unwanted, and presumably away from Bobby as well. But Bobby knew something was wrong and set off back to Edinburgh Grassmarket on his own, eventually finding Jock in a dirty passageway. The two of them spent the night in a seedy lodging house in Cowgate and slept on straw in the attic, but next day Jock could not be raised - he was dead. When he was buried in nearby Greyfriars churchyard, the Scotsman newspaper reported, "The dog, a Scotch terrier, was one of the most conspicuous mourners."

Three days after the funeral, at exactly 1 p.m. John Traill was taken aback when Bobby walked into the Dining Rooms half-starved, looking for food. He gave him a bone and the dog left. But Bobby returned the next day and this time John Traill followed him when he left and discovered him at the churchyard. He took Bobby back to his old farmer at Cauldbrae Farm, but soon afterwards the dog ran away again to the graveyard and, even though various people including John Traill tried to adopt him, Bobby howled until he was allowed back to Greyfriars churchyard. News spread of the terrier's extraordinary loyalty to the graveside of his dead shepherd - children fussed over him and people gathered outside the graveyard gates to watch the dog leave each day just before 1 p.m. to go to Traill's Dining Rooms for food.

For nine years this routine continued until the local authorities decided the law was being broken. Bobby was taken to court for being unlicensed and was declared a "vagrant". Traill was imprisoned for "harbouring" him, although the charge was later dismissed. The day after the court hearing, Bobby's whole story was reported in the "Scotsman" under the heading, "Strange Story of Dog," and when the Lord Provost of Edinburgh, William Chambers, read the article he adopted Bobby himself, paid his licence fee and gave him the freedom of the city and a new collar inscribed "Greyfriars Bobby, from the Lord Provost, 1867-licensed!".

There was no further news of Bobby until January 1872, when the "Scotsman" carried an obituary for him: "Many will be sad to hear that the poor but interesting dog, Greyfriars Bobby, died on Sunday evening. Every kind attention was paid to him in his last days by his guardian, Mr Traill, who has had him buried in a flower plot near Greyfriars church." A memorial statue of Greyfriars Bobby was commissioned and still stands today above a drinking-fountain on the corner of Candlemaker Row and George VI Bridge, and his special collar given by the Lord Provost is in the Huntly House Museum in Canongate. The grave of his master is now marked by a headstone erected by Bobby's American admirers, and although Mr Traill's Dining Rooms no longer exists it is commemorated at Number 6, Greyfriars Place with a brass plate on the door which reads, "Greyfriars Bobby was fed here 1858-1872."

(From "Pet Heroes" by Paul Simons)

COMPREHENSION (I)

1. What colour, and breed of dog was Greyfriars Bobby?
2. What was the name of Bobby's master?
3. What was his occupation, and where did he work?
4. Which day was market-day in Edinburgh?
5. At what time, and where, did Bobby and his master go to lunch?
6. When Bobby's master was sacked from his job where was he driven back to?
7. Explain in your own words the meaning of "sacked from his job".
8. What action did Bobby take when his master was driven away?
9. Explain the meaning of the word "seedy" in paragraph two.
10. Where did Bobby and his master spend the night?
11. Where was Jack buried?
12. Using your dictionary, give the meaning of "conspicuous" (paragraph 2).
13. John Traill was "taken aback". Rephrase this in your own words.
14. What condition was Bobby in when he walked into the Dining

Rooms?

15. When was Jock sacked from his job?
16. Where did Bobby find his master?
17. What did John Traill give to Bobby when he came to the Dining Rooms alone for the first time?
18. What did John Traill do the following day?
19. Various people, including John Traill, tried to adopt Bobby. Why were they all unsuccessful?
20. What effect did Bobby's behaviour have upon people?

COMPREHENSION (II) (slightly harder)

1. For how many years did Bobby continue his routine?
2. Who decided that the law was being broken?
3. What does "being unlicensed" mean, in the sense of the sentence?
4. What is a "vagrant"? You may use your dictionary.
5. Traill was put in prison for "harbouring" Bobby - in this sentence, what does "harbouring" mean?
6. Give another word (which keeps the sense of the sentence) for "dismissed". (In paragraph 4).
7. When was Bobby's story reported in "the Scotsman"?
8. Which important person read Bobby's story?
9. Bobby was given a new collar. What was inscribed upon it?
10. What three things did the important person do for Bobby?
11. When did Greyfriars Bobby die? Where was he buried? Who saw to this?
12. "Every kind attention" was paid to him. Rewrite this sentence in your own words.
13. What is an "obituary"? Find out from your dictionary. (Paragraph 5).
14. What is meant by a "memorial" statue? (Paragraph 5).
15. The statue was "commissioned". What does "commissioned" mean?
16. Where does the statue stand?
17. Where is Greyfriars Bobby's collar today?
18. Give the meaning of the word "commemorated".
19. Where is the brass plate, and what is written upon it?
20. Who was Greyfrairs Bobby's guardian? What is a guardian?

RECAPITULATION

(These exercises are more difficult)

1. State which of the following sentences contain SIMILES and which contain METAPHORS and explain the meaning of each one:

We were killing ourselves laughing.
I nearly died of embarrassment.
It was like being a candle in the midst of a fire work display.
She was grinning like a Cheshire cat.
He makes bullets for others to fire.
The critics tore the play to shreds.
The criminal fell into the detective's trap.
She felt as if her world was crumbling to dust.
The trouble with that young man is, his body has gone to his head.
The squadron kept an eye on all invasion points.

2. Which HOMOPHONE should be used to fill the blank spaces in the following sentences?

Buckingham Palace is the ________ of the Queen. (residents, residence).
I wear glasses because I have such poor ________. (site, sight).
She is beautiful, but unfortunately, she is also ________. (vane, vein, vain).
I like to dip toast into the ________ of a boiled egg. (yoke, yolk).
I need your ________ on this matter. (advise, advice).
The ________ of Everest was a thrilling event. (assent, ascent).
I don't know which prize to ________. (chews, choose).
The space probe was a stunning ________ of engineering. (feet, feat).
Are you coming to the village ________. (fate, fete).
Bring your books with you, you will ________ them. (knead, need).

3. Rewrite the following sentences, underlining the Auxiliary Verbs:

I might take my dog for a walk.
I should check whether my car needs petrol.
I may stroll down to the shops later.

I have measured how much material I need.
I am making a casserole for tea.
She was answering the doorbell when the telephone rang.
You must write a letter to your friend.
Will you tell me the answer tomorrow?
I will wash my car this afternoon.
Whilst my friend keeps me company I will clean my bedroom.

4. Combine the following pairs of sentences by using relative Pronouns:

a) Emma hurried back to the shop. She had left her purse in it.
b) I took my visitor to Culloden Moor. The Jacobites fought a battle there.
c) The speaker referred to Dirk Bogarde. Many beautiful adjectives were to be found in his books.
d) Sophie received no reply from the man. She sent him an application for a job.
e) The explorers came to a swamp. They had to pass through it to reach their goal.
f) We were shown a cottage. Shakespeare once lived there.
g) A storm destroyed the railway bridge. It spans the river.
h) The policeman returned the purse to its owner. Her name was inside.
i) The scouts did lots of odd jobs for the farmer. They camped in his field.
j) The old man revisited the town. He had been born there.

(Remember you may need to slightly re-arrange the words, and turn certain personal pronouns into relative pronouns and omit some personal pronouns).

5) Give one word for the following: (This is quite a difficult vocabulary question and unless you know the word you want a dictionary is of no use. To help you find the answers, I have given you the first three letters of each word).

Centralised government by officials. (Par)
The exclusive right to trade in something. (Con)

One who hates mankind. (Mis)
An agreement reached by mutual concession. (Com)
Wishing ill to others. (Mal)
One who acts as a go-between or peacemaker. (Med)
Speech or writing in praise of someone. (Eul)
Drugged and shipped as a sailor. (Pre)
One who does not believe in God. (Ath)
Medicine used to counteract poison or disease. (Ant)

6) Rewrite the following paragraph, changing it from indirect to direct speech. You must use inverted commas wherever necessary and change the past tense to the present tense; you will need to alter the personal pronouns, remember.

Mr Pearson said it was the finest sight he had ever seen in his life. He wouldn't have missed it for anything. He had been feeling very low that last week and it had done him good. He bade Smith not to talk nonsense about leaving the ship. He wouldn't lose him for anything after that, but if Smith liked to ship a fresh mate and crew he could please himself. If Smith would only come up to the house and let Mrs. Pearson see him, he, Pearson, would give him a couple of pounds. He begged Smith to get his hat and come.

7) The word "infer" means "deduce" or "draw a conclusion from".
The word "imply" means "insinuate" or "hint". For example:

From the look on his mother's face, John inferred that she had heard about the broken window.
Emma implied her distrust of her room-mate by locking her wardrobe.

Give the correct form of the words infer or imply to complete the blanks in the following sentences:
Since the others turned their backs on him, Tom _________ that they had not forgiven him for the trick he had played.
The teacher _________ by his look that he did not believe the boy's story.
In view of the expensive present she received on her birthday, Fiona _________ that her Godmother was very fond of her.
When we see a flag flying at half-mast, it is reasonable to_________ that someone has died.

Although the stranger spoke no English, he_________ his willingness to help by nodding his head vigorously.

WATERSHIP DOWN

They met with no more adventures that night, moving quietly along the edges of the fields under the dim light of a quarter-moon. The half-darkness was full of sounds and movement. Once Acorn put up a Plover, which flew round them, calling shrilly, until at length they crossed a bank and left it behind. Soon after, somewhere near them, they heard the unceasing bubbling of a Night-jar; a peaceful sound, without menace, which died gradually away as they pushed on. And once they heard a Corncrake calling as it crept among the long grass of a path verge. (It makes a sound like a human finger-nail drawn down the teeth of a comb.) but Elil they met none and although they were continually on the watch for signs of an Efrafan Patrol, they saw nothing but mice, and a few hedgehogs hunting for slugs along the ditches.

(From "Watership down" by Richard Adams)

COMPREHENSION

1) We are told the name of only one of the rabbits, in this passage. What is it?
2) Which three birds are mentioned in the passage?
3) Name two kinds of animals the rabbits saw.
4) What route did the rabbits take?
5) "But Elil they met none." What kind of animals do you think Elil may have been?
6) What were the hedgehogs hunting?
7) What sound is made by a CornCrake?
8) Give one example of Simile from the passage.
9) How does the author describe the sound of a night-jar?
10) One of the rabbits "put up" a plover. What does "put up" mean in this sentence?
11) This passage is rich in Prepositions. Make a list of all the prepositions contained in it.
12) How many <u>different</u> prepositions has the writer used?

13) Which Preposition is used most often?
14) Which sentence contains five Prepositions?
15) What was it that the rabbits were "on the watch for"?
16) Give five words from the passage which help to create the quiet atmosphere of the night.
17) Which phrase tells us that the rabbits were safe that night?
18) Give four adverbs from the passage.
19) Give eight nouns from the passage and state which two are proper nouns.
20) Make a list of ten nouns from the passage.

RECAPITULATION

1) Give one word for each of the following:

A room made largely of glass, joined to a house.
A building in which manufacturing takes place.
Tables, chairs, desks, bookcases, sofas etc.
A number of Congressmen.
A building where people go to keep fit.
A machine which dispenses drinks and chocolate.
A skirt worn by a Scotsman.
The nationality of a person who lives in Holland.
A male swan.
A light, strappy shoe worn in the summer.

2) Rewrite the following sentences and underline the Prepositions:

I have divided the property in accordance with your instructions.
The law according to God's word.
I am well aware of your mischief!
He was angered by her constant nagging.
Compared with Justin, Clive is quite noisy.
In looks, Emma is different from Sophie.
This dress is similar to yours.

She had an income independent of her job.
He is bound to rebel against such strict parents.
As for the future, it depends upon my exam results.

3) The following Proverbs have become "mixed". Rewrite them correctly:

People who live in glass houses - you cannot make an omelette!
An Englishman's word keeps the doctor away.
An apple a day is his bond.
Shouldn't throw stones without breaking eggs.
One man's meat is as good as a rest.
A change is another man's poison.
He who laughs last gathers no moss.
Rome was not built like success.
A rolling stone laughs longest.
Nothing succeeds in a day.

4) Two words which are often confused are "lend" and "borrow". If I LEND you my bicycle, you will be BORROWing it from me. Rewrite the following sentences using the words "lend" or "borrow" to fill the blank spaces: (You may need to add -er or -ing).

Please, would you_________ me your ruler?
I have forgotten mine, and need to_________ one.
I will promise to return your book tomorrow if you will_________ it to me tonight.
I feel guilty,_________ your clothes.
I don't mind_________ them to you, because I know you will return them.
Neither a_________ nor a _________ be.
I_________ so many pens to people that I don't have one to use myself.
People_________ because they do not provide themselves with their own equipment.
I have lost my purse, could you_________ me some money, please?
I hate_________ books. People never return them.

5) Rewrite the following sentences, inserting all the missing capital letters

and Punctuation:

it is late i am tired hungry and i want to go home
oh toby said mrs brown what a clever little dog you are
my friend said im really envious of your roller blades, i wish i had some like yours
would you like to borrow them i asked her
she thanked me but said that she would rather not borrow them
mother asked havent you finished the washing-up yet
the old man was very surprised he shook his head and said well i never
good gracious cried the old lady whatever are you doing now
so then what did he say i asked
there there its all better now the mother murmured to her tearful child

6) The following sentences contain misplaced words or phrases. Rewrite them correctly:

A large car passed along the road killing a dog containing two men.
I saw the town hall walking across the road.
The lady sent a table to her daughter with twisted legs.
I saw that our netball team played well in the newspaper.
The thunderstorm came on just as we reached home with unusual violence.
The shopkeeper noticed the broken window going through his shop.
A plot of land for sale by an estate agent a hundred feet long.
The family left the hotel where they had spent their holiday in a car.
Did you notice the grandfather clock rushing up the stairs?
There was a house by the sea out of which crept a baby.

7) Rewrite the following sentences underlining the Nouns in each and say what kind of noun:

A rolling stone gathers no moss.
Jack and Jill went up the hill.
Honesty is the best policy.
A swarm of bees in May, is worth a load of hay.
Manners make the man.
The plaza was a scene of gaiety.

Paris is the capital of France.
Like father, like son.
A huge flock of sheep.
Chopin was a very famous composer.

Part 5

SPELLING

SPELLING CONTENTS

H	C sounding like S	OVE sounding like UV	GH sounding like F
G	B	EA sounding like EE	N

DOUBLED CONSONANTS:

B C D F G L M N P R S T Z

SPELLING
(A WORD TO PARENTS)

During many years of teaching English, in mainstream classes and in Remedial classes, I have found that children find spellings much easier to learn when the words are listed in "families". That is, when there is some common link between all the words in a list, rather than a list of totally random and unconnected words. Indeed, to children who are experiencing learning difficulties with English, and in particular, dyslexic children, lists of random words can appear frightening and induce a kind of mental panic. On the other hand, a list of words which all end in ____ment (for example) are less daunting and seen to be manageable.

I would suggest that you give your child a list of 20 words at the most, to learn each week. This should be done by writing out <u>each</u> <u>word</u> three times <u>each</u> <u>day</u>.

The aim is for each of the 20 words to have been written 10 times by the end of the full week. For the child to write the first 3 words ten times on Monday, the second 3 words ten times on Tuesday, and so on, will not work half so well, as the child may easily have forgotten the first 3 words by the time Sunday comes! Writing all 20 words 3 times on Monday, 3 times on Tuesday and so on, all the way through the week, is far more effective. This way the child learns the spellings thoroughly, and the spellings stay learnt!

Confidence is the key to success with spelling. Once a child knows that he has learnt 20 spellings, he will feel a (necessary) sense of achievement. This will spur him on to learn the next 20 spellings and so on. Test the week's spellings only when you are reasonably sure he'll get most of them right. Give them to him in a random order, not in the order he's been writing them all week, this way you will know that he has really learnt each word and is not just remembering the order they come in.

It is very important to give the child lots of praise when he has successfully learnt his list, equally, play down any failures. As long as he's managed to learn <u>some</u> correctly, he knows more spellings than he did before, and nobody expects him to get them all right, every week, do they?

Stress that no-one can do better than their best. Even 2 correct spellings are 2 up on last week! He hasn't failed 18, he's succeeded with 2. The other 18 will come, maybe next week. There is NO RUSH. Keep the whole approach positive. Children "pick up" on negativity very quickly and take failure to heart quite drastically.

I cannot stress enough how important it is to praise, to build confidence, to give reassurance and to provide that essential feeling of achievement. There is a great deal of truth in the old saying "nothing succeeds like success" when it comes to giving children confidence in themselves. Please try not to show impatience; you haven't always been able to spell, yourself. You had to learn, as we all had to learn, and remarks of the...."You should know these, these are easy".... variety do NOT help at all. They can be downright destructive. On the other hand, to say occasionally...."I had an awful job learning spelling myself".... or ...."You did well to learn these spellings, they're really hard ones!".... can provide enormous relief and reassurance.

The following lists of spellings are only intended as a guide. Obviously there is not room enough here for a comprehensive guide to English spelling, but the lists should provide for most of your child's spelling needs. Some lists do not contain twenty words, and some contain a great many more because there is such a wealth of example. In those cases, pick out twenty words to use and save the rest for a different week, or just talk about them, their spelling, their meaning - and discard them. Some words appear in more than one list (knight in 'silent K' , also in 'GHT endings') necessarily, this will reinforce the learning of the word and does not matter.

By learning groups of twenty spellings of particular "families", your child cannot be guaranteed always to be able to spell any unfamiliar word he may be confronted with, but nine times out of ten, he will get it right.

On the whole, I have tried to avoid spelling "rules". Likewise reasons for why some consonants double, whilst some do not, and so on and so forth. The rules and reasons mean little to children, complicate matters and are, for our purposes, largely irrelevant anyway. The old "I before E except after C" rule is a prime example. It is totally misleading since there are almost as many words spelled "E before I." Therefore, I decided simply to provide straightforward lists of spellings to be learnt, which, if they are all worked through gradually, should provide your child with a good basic knowledge of English spelling. Some of the words in the lists may be unfamiliar to your child. Urge him to look up their meaning in a dictionary. In this way he will expand his vocabulary.

Finally, when you notice spelling mistakes in your child's school-work, try to resist the temptation to give him a list of corrections to learn, because if you do this we're back to the unconnected, unrelated list. Instead, make a note of each wrongly-spelt word, find several similar words (hopefully in the following lists) and give them to him to learn gradually, in "families". By the end of term you will find that he is no longer making mistakes with those particular words, and you and your child will both see a very marked improvement in his work.

PREFIXES

DIS -

disability disagree disallow disappear
disappoint disapprove disarm disarray
disassociate disaster disband disbelieve
disburse discard discern discharge
disciple discipline disclaim disclose
discolour discomfort disconnect disconsolate
discount discord discontinue discount
discourage discourse discourteous discover
discriminate discrepancy discreet discredit
discuss disdain disease disembark
disfavour disentangle disengage disenchant
disfigure disgorge disgrace disguise
dishonour dishonest dishearten disgust
disillusion disincline disinfect disinherit
dislocate dislike disinterest disintegrate
dislodge disloyal dismal dismantle
dismay dismiss dismount disobedient
disorder disorganize disown disorientate
disparage disparate dispatch dispel
display displace disperse dispensary
displease dispose dispossess disprove
disquiet disqualify dispute disproportion
disregard disrepair disreputable disrespect
dissent dissect dissatisfy disrupt
dissimilar dissipate dissociate dissolve
distil distemper distaste distance
distinct distinguish distort distract
district distribute distress distraught
distrust disturb disuse

CON -

concave	conceive	concert	conciliate
concomitant	concur	condescend	conduit
conference	confident	conflagration	confront
congest	conifer	connect	conquest
consecrate	conservation	consist	consort
constant	constitute	consul	contact
contemplate	content	continent	contour
contraption	contribute	controversy	convenient
converse	conceal	concentrate	concertina
concise	concord	concuss	condition
confection	confess	confine	conflict
confuse	congratulate	conjecture	connive
conscience	consecutive	conservatory	consolation
conspicuous	constellation	constrain	consult
contagious	contemporary	contest	contingent
contraband	contrary	contrite	convalesce
convent	convince	concede	concept
concerto	conclude	concourse	condemn
condone	confederate	confetti	confirm
conform	congeal	congregate	conjunction
connoisseur	conscious	consent	consider
consolidate	conspiracy	consternation	constrict
consume	contain	contempt	context
continue	contract	contrast	contrive
convection	conventional	convey	conceit
concern	concession	concoct	concrete
condense	conduct	confer	confident
confiscate	confound	congenial	congress
conjure	conquer	conscript	consequent
consign	consonent	constable	constituent
construct	consumption	contaminate	contend
contiguous	contortionist	contradict	contravene
control	convene	converge	convoy

PRO -

probable proboscis procession prodigious
proffer profound progress proliferate
prominent prompt propaganda proper
prophet proposal propulsion prospect
protect protestant protractor provender
province provoke proximity probate
procedure proclaim prodigy proficient
profuse prohibit prologue promise
prone propagate property propitiate
propound prosaic prosper protege
protocol protrude proverb provision
prow proxy probation proceed
procure produce profile progeny
project prolong promontory pronoun
propel prophecy propitious proprietary
prose prostrate protein prototype
proud provide provisional prowess
prudent problem process prodigal
profession profit programme projector
promenade promote pronounce propensity
prophesy proportion propriety prosecute
protagonist protest protract prove
providence proviso prowl

PRE -

preach preamble precarious precaution
precede precedent precept precinct
precious precipice precipitate precis
precise precision prelude precocious
precognition preconceive precursor predatory
predecessor predestine predetermine predicament
predicate predict predispose predominate
pre-eminent preen prefabricate preface

prefect	prefer	preference	prefix
preform	prehistoric	prejudge	prejudice
preliminary	prelude	premature	premeditate
premier	premise	premium	premonition
preoccupation	preparation	prepay	preponderance
preposition	prepossess	preposterous	prerequisite
prerogative	presage	prescient	prescribe
prescription	preselective	presence	present
presentation	preservation	preserve	preside
president	pressure	pressing	prestige
presume	presumption	pre-suppose	pretence
pretext	prevail	prevalent	prevaricate
prevent	preview	previous	prey

UN -

UN can prefix every verb, many nouns and many adjectives. It can form new adjectives and can also be an adverb, a preposition or a conjunction. As this prefix is unlimited in use, it is impossible to list it here entirely. Therefore the following list is simply a selection:

uncomplicated	untaught	under	undetected
unless	unsteady	unreliable	unmistakable
unkempt	unstable	undamaged	unexamined
unloved	unintentional	unappreciated	unrecognizable
until	untruth	uncovered	unscientific
unto	unsightly	uncurtained	unscheduled
unpleasant	unfading	uncertain	unprincipled
unload	unfaithful	unsure	unproductive
ungainly	unyielding	uncritical	unobjectionable
untidy	unearned	uncooked	unknown
undress	unkind	unconnected	unbending
underneath	unabashed	unattended	unused

IR -

iron
irate
irascible
iridescent
irksome
ironic
irretrievable
irrigate
ironmonger
irony
irradiate
irrational
irreconcilable
irrecoverable
irreverent
irritable
irredeemable
irrefutable
irregular
irrelevant
irreparable
irreplaceable
irreversible
irritate
irreproachable
irrepressible
irresistible
irresolute
irrespective
irresponsible
irrevocable

CIRCUM -

circumference
circumlocution
(circus)
circumflex
circumspect
circumnavigate
circumstance
circumscribe
circumvent

AUTO -

automation
autobahn
autobiography
autocrat
autogiro
autograph
autoharp
automatic
autosuggestion
automobile
autonomy
autopsy

SUB -

subdue
subject
subjugate
sublime
submarine
submerge
suburb
sublimate
submerse
submission
submit
subordinate
subscribe
subsequent
subvert
suborn
subservient
subside
subsidiary
subsidize
subsist
substance
subaltern
submersion
substantial
substantiate
substitute
subterfuge
subtle
subtract
subjacent

IM -

image	immature	immobilize	immune
imaginative	immeasurable	immodest	immunize
imbecile	immediate	immortal	immure
imbibe	immemorial	immovable	impale
imbue	immense	impact	impassable
imitate	immerse	impair	impassive
immaculate	immigrate	impart	impatient
immaterial	imminent	impartial	impeccable
impecunious	impede	impediment	impel
impend	impenetrable	imperative	imperceptible
imperfect	imperil	impermanent	impersonal
impersonate	impertinent	impervious	impetuous
impetus	implant	implement	implicate
implicit	implore	imply	impolite
import	important	importune	impose
impossible	imposter	impoverish	impound
impress	imprint	imprison	improbable
improper	improve	improvident	improvise
imprudent	impudent	impugn	impulse

MIS -

misadventure	miser	mission	misgiving
misanthropist	misery	missionary	mis-shapen
misbehave	miserable	mistake	miscarry
miscellaneous	mislead	mistrust	misfire
mischief	misogynist	misfit	misfortune
misconduct	misplace	misunderstand	misguided
misdemeanour	misprint	misuse	mishandle
mistletoe	mischance	mistral	misread
misapply	missing	missive	mister
misapprehend	missile	misdeed	mistress

IN -

inability
inaccurate
inadequate
inadvertant
inane
inappropriate
inferno
influence
inhabit
insincere
install
intelligent
interview

inaudible
incapable
incessant
incident
include
incognito
infinitive
inform
injection
insolent
instruct
intend
intrigue

intolerable
inconvenient
indefinite
indicate
indigent
indistinct
indivisible
infinite
infuriate
injustice
insomnia
instrument
interest

industrious
inept
inevitable
infectious
infer
inferior
inflict
inherit
insert
inspire
instinct
intervene
invisible

ILL -

illusion
illegal
illegible
illicit

illiterate
illness
illogical
illegitimate

illuminate
illusive
illustrate
illustrious

TRA -

trace
track
tract
tractable
traction
tractor
trade
tradition
trafalgar
transit

traffic
tragedy
tragic
trail
trailer
train
translucent
traipse
trait
transmit

traitor
trajectory
tram
trammel
tramp
trample
trampoline
trance
tranquil
transparent

transact
transcend
transcribe
transfer
transfix
transform
transfuse
transient
translate
traveller

WORD ENDINGS OR SUFFIXES

-URE ENDINGS

literature	overture	furniture	adventure
secure	endure	cure	sure
lure	pure	torture	picture
capture	mature	impure	unsure
treasure	pleasure	measure	leisure
pressure	fissure	allure	assure
impure	displeasure	reassure	insecure

-ABLE ENDINGS

comfortable	affordable	reasonable	climbable
probable	eatable	drinkable	laughable
syllable	rideable	disable	able
washable	table	stable	unstable
unreasonable	questionable	laudable	miserable

-DGE ENDINGS

ledge	edge	hedge	dodge
lodge	badge	wedge	nudge
fudge	sludge	sledge	knowledge
pledge	sedge	dredge	cadge
budge	midge	ridge	

-TH ENDINGS

beneath	underneath	earth	worth
with	teeth	both	bath

death	moth	breath	

-CIOUS ENDINGS

gracious	ungracious	delicious	officious
luscious	suspicious	spacious	voracious
veracious	mendacious	audacious	capacious
fallacious	malicious	vicious	precious
conscious	unconscious	subconscious	precocious

-IDE ENDINGS

abide	decide	confide	wide
inside	deride	collide	co-incide
reside	outside	side	suicide
cyanide	divide	guide	hide
ride	tide	betide	beside
slide			

-IRE ENDINGS

fire	bonfire	require	inquire
enquire	desire	sire	shire
spire	retire	inspire	expire
wire	ire	mire	dire
hire	eire	tire	esquire

-ICE ENDINGS

voice	choice	twice	ice
lice	mice	slice	dice
nice	rice	entice	juice

price	vice	thrice	sluice
splice	trice	police	chalice
malice	office	orifice	suffice
rejoice	advice		

-ISE ENDINGS

precise	concise	wise	cruise
poise	rise	revise	advertise
noise	incise	chastise	exercise
despise	excise	surprise	reprise
disguise	unwise	prise	advise

-GHT ENDINGS

In all these words, both the 'g' and the 'h' are silent.

sight	fraught	wrought	light
freight	might	overwrought	fought
caught	fight	slight	height
flight	twilight	midnight	sought
sleight	eight	weight	right
fright	bought	nought	brought
night	alight	delight	alright

-AY ENDINGS

tray	holiday	splay	clay
pray	repay	delay	okay
play	say	way	Monday
day	stray	spray	pay
may	sway	relay	bay
hay	lay	away	gay

ray	display	gray	hurray

-LLY ENDINGS

usually	beautifully	silly	jolly
actually	faithfully	fully	wholly
gradually	wonderfully	holly	squally
finally	really	joyfully	carefully
hilly	bully	woolly	occasionally

The suffixes (endings) -sion and -tion are both used to denote Abstract Nouns. As they are pronounced alike it is sometimes difficult to decide which a word ends in. The following lists are for you to learn gradually, you will then find it easier to decide which is the correct ending when you use a word which is new or unfamiliar to you.

-SION ENDINGS

revision	possession	illusion	vision
remission	fusion	television	occasion
precision	decision	omission	diversion
mission	confusion	ascension	session
incision	impulsion	passion	delusion
perversion	immersion	derision	diffusion
aversion	conversion	permission	

-TION ENDINGS

destination	situation	conversation	nation
attention	direction	station	ration
action	relation	caution	investigation
mention	portion	operation	exertion

lotion	pretention	devotion	vexation
convention	resolution	discretion	dissention
exemption	redemption	hallucination	

-CK ENDINGS

black	track	block	flock
flick	wreck	sock	sack
sick	knock	knack	clock
back	frock	mock	shock
wrack	crack	shack	lack
lock	dock	neck	peck
whack	slack	kick	lick

-ECT ENDINGS

respect	circumspect	recollect	collect
connect	disconnect	reflect	dialect
select	infect	disinfect	suspect
reject	detect	correct	direct
sect	protect	eject	dissect
insect	inject	defect	affect
effect	disaffect		

-EDE ENDINGS

concede	recede	impede	accede
stampede	swede	suede	

-ODE ENDINGS

explode	implode	diode	mode
code	anode	erode	lode
ode	electrode	cathode	strode

-END ENDINGS

recommend	spend	send	end
friend	lend	wend	pretend
fend	contend	amend	distend
stipend	commend	dividend	suspend
fiend	Ostend	trend	depend
defend	befriend	offend	extend

-ENT ENDINGS

permanent	tent	recent	decent
current	compliment	complement	decadent
represent	present	lament	comment
scent	dependent	convent	talent
salient	confident	accident	accomplishment
incipient	recipient	imminent	eminent
clement	inclement	implement	rent
lent	spent	sent	went
consent	dissent	mis-spent	frequent
independent	content	rodent	bent
diligent	moment	silent	latent
portent	patent	patient	ornament

-ANT ENDINGS

distant	currant	pleasant	pheasant
peasant	reliant	pliant	plant
rant	elephant	chant	defiant
deviant	ant	scant	decant
militant	valiant	brilliant	triumphant
giant	grant	want	recant
mutant	descant	mordant	extant
commandant	discordant	dependant	dormant
implant	transplant	croissant	savant
servant	cormorant	tenant	pennant

-IAL ENDINGS

genial	denial	dial	phial
menial	cordial	remedial	sartorial
memorial	facial	racial	superficial
official	palatial	special	martial
partial	impartial	circumstantial	trial
substantial	proverbial	bestial	beneficial
social	perennial	aerial	serial
trivial	convivial	vial	

-OSE ENDINGS

bellicose	morose	loose	lose
verbose	noose	moose	dispose
repose	rose	nose	goose
pose	disclose	close	compose
depose	suppose	lactose	fructose
sucrose	glucose	expose	comatose
those	whose	chose	impose
enclose			

-ST ENDINGS

resist
quest
guest
pest
consist
nest
conquest
foremost
crest
jest
ghost

capitalist
rest
digest
post
persist
cost
forest
first
worst
gust
host

list
mist
ingest
coast
cyst
frost
chest
thirst
mast
behest
lest

gist
moist
request
desist
elastoplast
bequest
infest
crust
blast
aghast
interest

-ING ENDINGS

something
ring
bring
Herring
skirting
string
everything
railing
Waxwing
Gosling

anything
sing
sting
netting
fling
spring
clothing
paling
Redwing
costing

nothing
swing
sibling
coating
ceiling
darling
farthing
offspring
wedding

earring
cling
king
fleeting
thing
yearling
Starling
Bunting
bedding

-OW ENDINGS

borrow
marrow
callow
yellow
narrow

tomorrow
barrow
hollow
follow
Moscow

blow
sallow
bellow
fellow
tallow

sorrow
meadow
below
fallow
Mallow

mellow	shadow	meiow	know
glow	vow	now	show
sow	tow	flow	row
crow	how	grow	cow

-NCE ENDINGS

since	prince	prance	dance
trance	chance	glance	hence
fence	whence	coincidence	balance
valance	silence	pittance	wince
lance	mince	once	quince
dunce	convince	denounce	flounce
trounce	fragrance	announce	providence

LETTER COMBINATIONS

DOUBLE E

feet	weep	speed	sleet
meet	greet	meek	seek
cheeky	sweet	fleeting	flee
reed	weed	creed	deed
seed	keep	deep	street
sheet	Leeds	cheese	freeze
squeeze	free	indeed	misdeed
teeth	feel	greed	Greece
fleece	tree	between	screen
sheen	teething	sweeten	greeting

DOUBLE O

wool	fool	soot	boot
loot	shoot	toot	loom
doom	gloom	soon	room
balloon	foot	cool	stool
pool	spool	school	tool
cartoon	moon	croon	swoon
wood	good	hood	mood
Rangoon	food	blood	brood
flood	stood	spittoon	ballroom

EXC - WORDS

excess	excite	exclaim	excavate
Excalibur	excise	exclude	exclusive
excel	excellent	excrete	exceed

excruciating	except	exception	excerpt
exchange	exchequer	excursion	excuse

QU WORDS

There is no word in our English language which contains Q without an immediately following U.

quick	queen	queue	quiver
Quebec	require	request	enquire
inquire	squire	esquire	squirrel
quest	bequest	question	quiz
quarry	quack	quantity	quality
query	quay	relinquish	squeeze
squid	squash	squeek	squeal
sequel	squawk	sequence	consequence
squall	technique	unique	antique
mystique	risque	racquet	bouquet
quite	quiet	quart	requiem
square	quaint	quarter	quaver

TH IN THE MIDDLE

other	brother	bother	weather
either	neither	breathe	heather
leather	teething	nothing	mother
father	whether	together	clothing
loathing	farthing		

GHT IN THE MIDDLE

sighted	lighten	heighten	frighten
alighted	mighty	weighty	nightie

eighty	eighteen	fighting	naughty
delighted	delightful	slightly	rightful
sighting	thoughtful	slighted	nightingale
flighty	almighty	frightful	frightening
mightiful	brightly	laughter	daughter

AI WORDS

paid	main	rail	stairs
sail	wait	against	chair
Spain	chain	paint	pair
plain	maid	again	remain
refrain	claim	exclaim	reclaim
regain	sustain	rain	wain
maiden	swain	gain	faith
faithful	faithless	stain	complain

IE WORDS

relief	chief	sieve	lied
belief	handkerchief	grieve	died
thief	achieve	cried	friend
believe	relieve	tried	tied
fried	pied	hurried	worried
scurried	carried	vied	espied
married	buried	bullied	sullied
friend	grief	diesel	denied

EI WORDS

their	weir	either	neither
eight	eighty	eighteen	weight
weighty	freight	neigh	sleigh

weigh
reign
rein
reinstate
deign
Eider

sleight
seize
reimburse
reissue
de-icer
eiderdown

leisure
seizure
reindeer
reincarnate
feign
Eisteddfod

sovereign
seismic
reinforce
deity
feint

EI AFTER C

conceive
receive

ceiling
perceive

deceive
conceit

OULD WORDS

could
would

should
boulder

shoulder
mould

ST WORDS

question
sticky
paste
pastel
disaster
elastoplast
nestle
costly
Leicester
obstruction

bastion
starve
waste
mystery
restore
listen
pestle
congestion
Chesterfield
obstinate

station
hasty
instinct
history
master
glisten
hostel
digestion
frosting
procrastinate

festival
nasty
postal
plaster
sister
christened
hostelry
resistance
instruction
fasten

PH WORDS

pharmacy	pheasant	phobia	nymph
philosophy	telephone	stereophonic	samphire
microphone	sapphire	phantom	phonetic
sphere	orphan	symphony	graph
physical	trophy	photography	phase
phrase	morphine	diphtheria	elephant
telegraph	metaphor	phosphorescent	phonic
Phoenix	phoney	phosphate	physician
physics	physique	sphinx	biography

AU WORDS

authentic	author	authority	autobiography
autograph	automatic	automobile	auxiliary
aught	augment	auditor	audition
auction	auburn	audacious	audible
audience	auditorium	auspicious	naughty
haughty	daughter	haul	taught
caught	fault	because	laugh
cause	plausible	Autumn	August
chauffeur	aunt	Australia	caustic

ID WORDS

livid	turgid	stupid	horrid
torrid	corridor	void	limpid
rapid	candid	rid	mid
avoid	steroid	skid	kid
pallid	squalid	invalid	valid
squid	aphid	rigid	avid
slid	acrid	grid	acid
placid	consider	timid	tidy

CY WORDS

cycle	bicycle	cynic	cyanide
bankruptcy	encyclopaedic	cyclone	Cyclops
cygnet	cylinder	cymbal	cypher
Cyprus	cypress	cyst	currency
secrecy	scythe	delicacy	

SCH WORDS

scheme	schooner	school	scholar
schedule	scholarship		

SILENT LETTERS

Letters which are crucial to the spelling of a word, but which are not pronounced are called "silent letters". Here are some examples:

SILENT K

knight	knave	knot	knickers
kneel	knee	knit	knowledge
knack	knuckle	knife	know
knock	knew	knapsack	knead
knell	knob		

SILENT H

When H is preceded by T or S it produces the "th" and "sh" sounds, but when it is preceded by W, the H is silent.

whack	whale	wharf	what
wheat	wheedle	wheel	whistle
wheeze	whelk	overwhelm	whelp
when	where	whet	whether
whey	which	whiff	while
whim	whimper	whimsical	whine
whip	whippet	whipsnade	whirr
whirl	whisk	whisker	whiskey
whisper	whist	whitsun	white
whittle	whizz	why	whoosh

SILENT G

When G is followed by N, whether at the beginning or the end of a word, the G is silent.

gnaw	gnu	sign
gnat	reign	align
gnome	benign	feign
gnash	resign	foreign
gnarled	design	

SILENT W

wreck	wrong	wrist	who
wrack	wring	wrench	whose
wrest	wriggle	wrought	whom
wrestle	wry	awry	whole

C SOUNDING LIKE S

civic	civil	circle	circular
city	cell	cellular	circumference
circus	cereal	certain	certainly
cycle	ice	icy	icicle
mice	dice	choice	voice
defence	fence	once	dance
danced	dancing	chance	lance
glance	chalice	palace	Alice
conference	inference	malice	sincere

SILENT B

succumb	womb	tomb	dumb

thumb	numb	climb	limb
jamb	crumb	lamb	comb
plumb	doubt	debt	

S SOUNDING LIKE Z

lose	fuse	refuse	confuse
use	cruise	choose	muse
shoes	toes	news	close
ease	please	cheese	chose
those	whose	these	reason
cousin	poison	miser	wise

OVE SOUNDING LIKE UV

above	love	dove	glove
oven	coven	cover	shove
shovel			

EA SOUNDING LIKE EE

deal	heal	peal	meal
steal	seam	dream	cream
treat	heat	seat	bead
lead	seal	squeal	read
clean	stream	weave	leave
please	plead	peach	reach
mean	teach	heave	increase

Y SOUNDING LIKE I

sympathy	symphony	hypnotise	hypocrite

synonym	antonym	homonym	nymph
synchronise	system	hymn	synthetic
mystery	mythical	physical	dyslexic
crystal	tryst	cyst	hysterical
lynch	idyll	physician	hypnotic

GH SOUNDING LIKE F

rough	tough	trough	laugh
enough	cough	draughty	

SILENT N

hymn	Autumn	column
solemn	condemn	damn

DOUBLED CONSONANTS

B

bubble gobble gabble nobbly
wobble shabby hobby rabbit
nibble scribble bobbin cobbler
lobby flabby robber rubber
chubby tubby rabble dabble
hobble webbing stubble stubborn
squabble cobble

C

accept accede acclaim occupy
occult accumulate accord accordian
succour stucco success succinct
succulent succumb eccentric accelerate
accent accentuate access accessory
accident acclimatize accolade accommodate
accompany accomplice accomplish account
accurate accuse accustom

D

puddle daddy paddle waddle
coddle cuddle muddle middle
sudden hidden trodden giddy
midden meddle midday sodden
padding pudding adder ladder
bladder fiddle riddle addle
fodder odd muddy address
befuddle add addict addition

F

off	fluff	snuff	effluent
effect	affect	differ	different
efficient	effort	effusive	miff
muff	affair	affable	affection
affirm	affix	afflict	affluent
afford	offhand	coffee	boffin
toffee	waffle	snaffle	baffle
traffic	duffle	muffle	snuffle

G

smuggle	snuggle	gaggle	giggle
wriggle	nugget	waggle	wiggle
ragged	baggy	baggage	luggage
snigger	trigger	haggard	maggot
soggy	foggy	haggis	suggest

L

million	trillion	ballast	ball
wall	hall	fall	yell
yellow	mellow	Mallow	hollow
hello	Dallas	follow	thrill
trill	bill	will	gill
miller	collar	pillow	bellow
bell	tell	knell	billow
cellar	cellular	celluloid	cello
call	tall	small	willow
sallow	fallow	millet	collect
intellect	intelligent		

M

swimmer	hammer	comma	common
Summer	plummet	glimmer	pommel
mummy	hammock	shimmer	stammer
programme	gramme	grammar	tummy
simmer	chummy	yummy	Lemming
accommodation			

N

cannot	connect	pennant	whinney
bonnet	sonnet	rennet	Gannet
bunny	dinner	beginner	funny
Fennel	punnet	spinney	runner
sinner	spanner	banner	scanner
tunnel	funnel	flannel	kennel

P

apple	ripple	topple	tipple
happy	nappy	sopping	whopping
pepper	chopper	copper	dapper
flipper	slipper	clipper	sapphire
dropper	appear	disappear	reappear
puppy	supper	kipper	happen
whippet			

R

mirror	horror	warrior	carry
borrow	barrier	marry	merry

worry	hurry	scurry	Surrey
barrel	furry	sorry	tomorrow
barrow	corridor	warrant	warren
barren	currant	current	terror
terrific			

S

kiss	miss	hiss	hassle
dismiss	pass	lass	grass
mass	loss	posse	floss
gross	mess	chess	less
lesson	passion	Russian	mission
remission	permission	session	hessian
moss	glass	gloss	class
classic	Jurassic	regress	dress
undress	confess	redress	address

T

rattle	bottle	chatter	rotten
battle	fettle	natter	forgotten
kitten	kettle	letter	matter
mitten	nettle	better	batter
written	settle	cottage	clatter
shatter	shutter	butter	bitter
twitter	shuttle	mutter	stutter
jittery	lottery	pottery	patter
jotter	mettle	pattern	Bittern
glitter	litter	little	chattel
prattle	spittle	button	scuttle

Z

dizzy	whizz	buzz	fuzz
blizzard	gizzard	fizzy	dazzle
puzzle	guzzle	nozzle	drizzle
nuzzle	jazz	sizzle	grizzly
Buzzard	muzzle		

CONCLUSION
A word to the children

Well done! You have worked your way through the complete English course and now your grammar is perfect, your punctuation entirely correct and your spelling immaculate........isn't it?

Now you can confidently create your own writings. They may take the form of letters, stories or poems, but I know (don't I?) that these writings of yours will be full of carefully chosen adjectives and adverbs, precise nouns and verbs and original similes and metaphors.

Your creative writing will express your own thoughts and feelings, no one else's. You are unique and your own unique personality will shine through your writing. Never alter it, to make it like someone else's writing, because you will spoil the work that you created, which is special and does not deserve to be spoilt.

My aim when choosing the texts for the comprehension section was to provide a "taster" of interesting subjects and different styles of writing in the hope that one of them might prompt you to write your own story. Some of you may prefer to write a poem rather than a story, so to give you inspiration I asked John the Poet to write something for this book, because it has been said of his poetry that "This is the best poetry being written in English today." He wrote this poem for you. It is called

"Remedial English"

There was no need to be stern, but she was in front of her class,
As she told the children to tidy away the clay and sit ready to be told.
I was twenty-one: Sixteen years older than the children,
But like them, younger than the woman trying so hard to be old.

Night Sounds! Children! I want you to imagine!
The day is over! Tell me all the sounds that you hear at night.
I heard a chair leg make that noise with the chalk-dust on the floor,
That it makes as it stirs the motes in the beams and the sunlight.

Then she said "Good!" When I heard "Owls hooting."
And I saw her respond to the five year old mind
Trying to divine what it was she wanted to hear,
"Leaves rustling" was good too. She was pleased until she looked behind.

"Apples dropping from trees." smiled a boy and she frowned.
She wrote "Leaves rustling" and "Owls hooting" on the board.
"Night sounds. Night sounds! I asked for a Night sound."
Along with heaven's embroidered cloths of gold, the boy was ignored.

His dull thuds upon the moon, or altered by rain, still make the noise
Of evenings upon my pillow. And before the night I pray, waiting for sleep,
Wide awake, for the care of those angels who invite us to sail as boys
Listening to the apples, before we were taught to count sheep.